Beyond Fighter Escort

Beyond Fighter Escort

by

MAJ. JAMES F. BRUNO
U.S.A.F. RES (RET.)

Beyond Fighter Escort

ISBN No. 0-9648032-1-6

Library of Congress No. 95-70702

Ken Cook Co.
9929 West Silver Spring Dr.
P.O.Box 25267
Milwaukee, WI 53225

BEYOND FIGHTER ESCORT

TO MY WIFE
MERLYN
FOR HER TIRELESS WORK
OF EDITING, REWRITING AND BEING
MY PERSONAL LOVING ASSISTANT.

Introduction

Foreword by: H.B. Bankhead, Captain,
Delta Airlines, (Ret)

Table of Contents

Chapters

MAJOR GENERAL FAY R. UPTHEGROVE

Born January 28, 1905 • Died January 8, 1992
Graduated from West Point United States Military Academy
June 1927

Colonel Fay R. Upthegrove was the originator of the 99th Bomb Group (B-17). It was formed Sept. 1942. He also was the originator of the Diamond Box formation, he also insisted on a tight flying formation. That proved to save both men and planes from enemy planes and more bomb hits in target area.

During World War Two the 99th flew 395 Combat Missions from 1943 to 1945 out of Africa and Italy, in the Fifteenth Air Force. The group consisted of the 346, 347, 348, and the 416th Squadrons.

The 99th is still going strong. It went from B-17 to the Stealth Bomber of Desert Storm. It is now called the 99th Bomb Wing.

FOREWORD

by H. B. BANKHEAD

Captain, Delta Airlines, Retired

For 53 years I have had the good fortune of being associated with James Bruno, during six months of intensive combat training and 50 combat missions in the B-17 Flying Fortress out of North Africa during World War II. We have had the best of these many years of friendship and camaraderie. His graphic portrayal of events, both civilian and military leading to pilots wings is most interesting and informative.

Beyond Fighter Escort relives fascinating experiences of our combat crew of which I was first pilot and Lieutenant Bruno my co-pilot on some 44 missions. Other missions leading to his 50 missions were flown by him as first pilot or as co-pilot for other pilots. Our plane was appropriately named *The Persuader.* We were members of the original 99th Heavy Bombardment Group that played an important role in the defeat of German General Erwin Rommel and his Africa Corps.

The crew of *The Persuader* is grateful to James Bruno for bringing to us the fascinating experiences and interesting episodes of our training and close relationships we enjoyed as a team in our close-knit group of ten highly trained men in B-17's. Because of his kindness and concern for all, he was affectionately named "Mother Hen" of our crew.

Beyond Fighter Escort is indeed fascinating reading for anyone to learn how the heavy bombardment groups carried out the destruction of the Axis war machine during World War II.

ACKNOWLEDGEMENTS

THE AUTHOR AND PUBLISHER GRATEFULLY ACKNOWLEDGE THE COOPERATION AND PERMISSION TO QUOTE ARTICLES AND HISTORICAL RECORDS THAT HAVE MADE THIS BOOK POSSIBLE. OUR HEARTFELT THANKS FOR YOUR KINDNESS AND CONTRIBUTIONS.

MRS. W. R. BURRELL	OMAHA, NE
MAJ. GENERAL F.R. UTPHEGROVE (DECEASED)	GAUTIER, MS
LT. GENERAL F.H. GRISWOLD (SAC COMMAND)	OMAHA, NE
CAPT H.B. BANKHEAD (DELTA AIRLINES)	ATLANTA, GA
J. EDGAR HOOVER (DECEASED)	WASHINGTON, D.C.
MRS. MARIE DEVEREAUX	CUDAHY, WI
DEPT OF THE U.S. AIR FORCE	WASHINGTON, D.C.
STRATEGIC AIR COMMAND	OMAHA, NE
OMAHA WORLD HERALD	OMAHA, NE
ASSOCIATED PRESS WIRE PHOTO	NEW YORK, NY
THE MILWAUKEE JOURNAL	MILWAUKEE, WI
THE MILWAUKEE SENTINEL	MILWAUKEE, WI
NEWBURY WEEKLY NEWS	NEWBURY, BERKSHIRE, ENGLAND
WAUKESHA DAILY FREEMAN	WAUKESHA, WI

INTRODUCTION

Captain Harry R. Burrell, Squadron Commander, selected me to be his co-pilot when the 99th. heavy bomb group was formed in Boise, Idaho. Gowen Field was a B-17 training base to which I and 36 classmates were sent upon graduation from advanced twin engine that we completed at Roswell, New Mexico on September 29, 1942.

Harry is no longer with us, but his Mother's many scrapbooks of his accomplishments gave me the inspiration to write about the 99th Bomb Group. General Fay R. Upthegrove exchanged many letters with Harry. When I informed the General that I planned to write about the 99th, he suggested our Captain Fairbanks had a flair for writing and perhaps we could get together. I knew trying to locate him some 25 years later would not be an easy task.

Throughout the years of 1970 to 1974 I received historical photos of our bomb group for our 100 mission celebration in North Africa. Our B-17 group was the recipient of many awards for pinpoint bombing and tight formations. General Upthegrove also sent the history of the group upon completion of the 300th mission. I was privileged to obtain many letters he received. The letters revealed the love and respect the men had for their General.

The 99th Bomb Group that was formed in October, 1942 was to land in North Africa shortly after the invasion there led by Army General, Mark Clark.

FROM THE AUTHOR

The previous pages contain the acknowledgments secured from 1970 to 1974 when I decided to write about the 99th Heavy Bombardment Group. Major General Fay R. Upthegrove, during those years, furnished me with the history which is the hallmark of this book.

In September, 1994, I gave the manuscript to author, Lee Riordan, and left for our 99th Reunion at Hampton, Virginia. Upon our return, Merlyn and I found an endorsement which spurred us on. Lee is also a screen writer and writing instructor at Marquette University in Milwaukee. I was aware of the fact he was experiencing a problem with his sight. "I strained my eyes over your riveting material - really terrific" he wrote.

Dr. John H. Fredrickson of Cape Canaveral, Florida became my next critic and editor. He received his Ph.D. from the University of Wisconsin, Madison, and is an Educational Planner. He was tough, and informed me he would be so before I sent him the manuscript. "Potential fantastic, major rewrite imperative" was written across pages. Also, "Great!" and "Is this necessary?" "Weak, like a little old lady." "Nice. " "Very good." Thanks, John, you made my day!

Rejections? I've had a few. Only top publishers were sent the manuscript, or proposal. They were kind.... "This is not for us, you should find a smaller publisher." "It does not fit our niche." I struck out at four top publishers.

Then, I remembered my former employer of about 25 years earlier, Ken Cook Publishing Company, Milwaukee, Wisconsin. Ken, Jr. had screened the 25 photos sent to me by General Upthegrove. Ken was happy to see me and with a handshake and a "Gentlemen's Agreement," the book, "Beyond Fighter Escort," became a reality.

By 1945, the 99th had flown 395 combat missions. It was at the 99th Reunion at Rapid City, South Dakota in October, 1992 that I learned the 99th was one of the most decorated bomb groups of the war. Classmates, Marion J Larkin and Michael J. Yarina, hosted that reunion. Marion Larkin, a pilot, received his Distinguished Flying Cross 51 years late, in 1995.

The 99th had its presence at Ellsworth Air Force Base in Rapid City. They had complements of B-52's and the B-1 bomber. These aircraft participated in the Iraqi War in 1991.

Without a doubt, most everyone who participated in bombing the German and Italian targets has a story to relate of the daring escapes during air battles with the enemy.

The material from General Upthegrove, as well as personal observation in the right seat of the B-17, will captivate you in *"Beyond Fighter Escort."*

CHAPTER 1

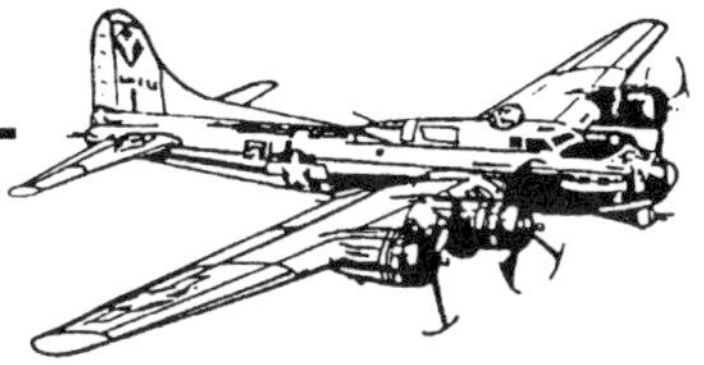

MISSING IN ACTION

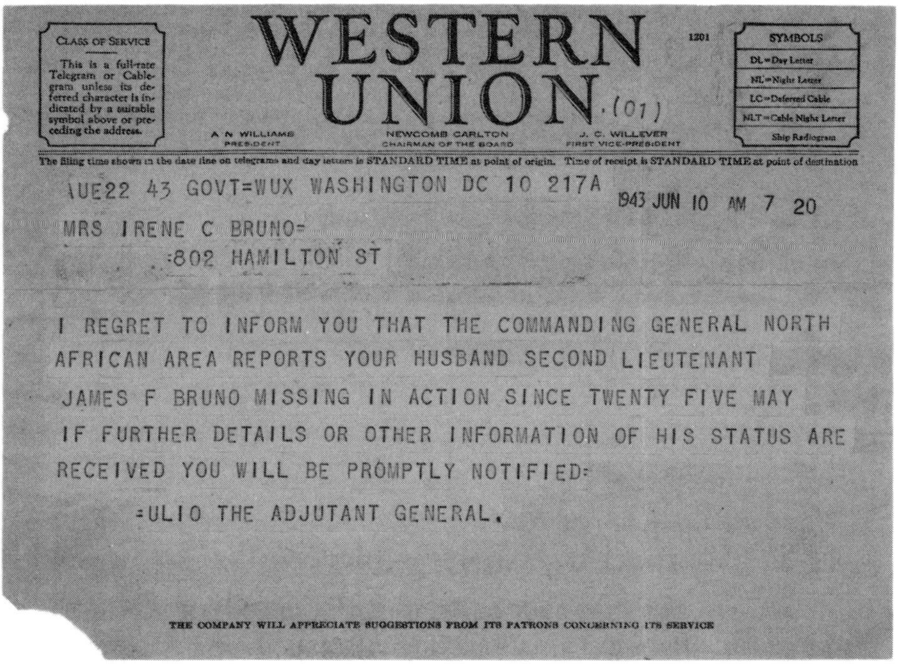

WESTERN UNION .(01)

CLASS OF SERVICE
This is a full-rate Telegram or Cablegram unless its deferred character is indicated by a suitable symbol above or preceding the address.

A N WILLIAMS PRESIDENT | NEWCOMB CARLTON CHAIRMAN OF THE BOARD | J. C. WILLEVER FIRST VICE-PRESIDENT

1201

SYMBOLS
DL = Day Letter
NL = Night Letter
LC = Deferred Cable
NLT = Cable Night Letter
Ship Radiogram

The filing time shown in the date line on telegrams and day letters is STANDARD TIME at point of origin. Time of receipt is STANDARD TIME at point of destination

\UE22 43 GOVT=WUX WASHINGTON DC 10 217A

1943 JUN 10 AM 7 20

MRS IRENE C BRUNO=
:802 HAMILTON ST

I REGRET TO INFORM YOU THAT THE COMMANDING GENERAL NORTH AFRICAN AREA REPORTS YOUR HUSBAND SECOND LIEUTENANT JAMES F BRUNO MISSING IN ACTION SINCE TWENTY FIVE MAY IF FURTHER DETAILS OR OTHER INFORMATION OF HIS STATUS ARE RECEIVED YOU WILL BE PROMPTLY NOTIFIED=

=ULIO THE ADJUTANT GENERAL.

THE COMPANY WILL APPRECIATE SUGGESTIONS FROM ITS PATRONS CONCERNING ITS SERVICE

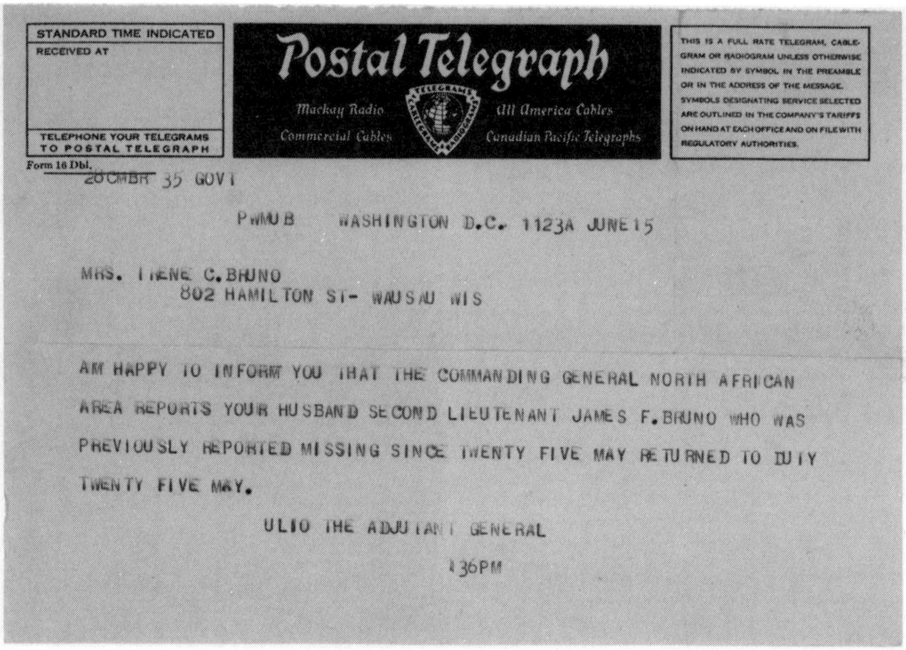

STANDARD TIME INDICATED
RECEIVED AT

TELEPHONE YOUR TELEGRAMS TO POSTAL TELEGRAPH

Postal Telegraph

Mackay Radio — All America Cables
Commercial Cables — Canadian Pacific Telegraphs

THIS IS A FULL RATE TELEGRAM, CABLEGRAM OR RADIOGRAM UNLESS OTHERWISE INDICATED BY SYMBOL IN THE PREAMBLE OR IN THE ADDRESS OF THE MESSAGE. SYMBOLS DESIGNATING SERVICE SELECTED ARE OUTLINED IN THE COMPANY'S TARIFFS ON HAND AT EACH OFFICE AND ON FILE WITH REGULATORY AUTHORITIES.

Form 16 Dbl.

20CMBH 35 GOVT

PWMUB WASHINGTON D.C. 1123A JUNE 15

MRS. IRENE C. BRUNO
802 HAMILTON ST- WAUSAU WIS

AM HAPPY TO INFORM YOU THAT THE COMMANDING GENERAL NORTH AFRICAN AREA REPORTS YOUR HUSBAND SECOND LIEUTENANT JAMES F. BRUNO WHO WAS PREVIOUSLY REPORTED MISSING SINCE TWENTY FIVE MAY RETURNED TO DUTY TWENTY FIVE MAY.

ULIO THE ADJUTANT GENERAL

136PM

Thanks, Adjutant General Ulio, what was the hurry?

Our crew happened to take a side trip on the way back to Africa.

Our number four engine propeller ran out of control when an anti-aircraft shell disabled the control. It soon melted out of the crankcase, cut the right aileron control cable and spun lazily into the Mediterranean from 10,000 feet. The group was out of sight, heading home to Africa.

We felt the need to ditch when the vibration made controlling difficult. A "MAYDAY" was sent out by our radio operator. The Germans best twin engine fighter bomber answered the message. It came with a fresh load of cannon and machine gun ammunition. After a few bursts, we decided to fight back. This pilot did not come to rescue our lonely trip home. We, 1st Lieutenant H. B. Bankhead and I, a Second Lieutenant, took him on for about twenty minutes. That delay caused us to use up precious fuel. Not able to return to base, we landed at the first sight of land. An Army truck completed the next 150 miles the next day.

I wanted to fly, and that is what put me into this situation. I saw Charles A. Lindberg fly over the family farm on August 22, 1927. That flight by the "Lone Eagle" was the spark that gave me the resolve to someday soar high in the skies. I wrote my High School career book on Aviation in 1937, ten years later. "Aviation," I wrote, "is in its infancy. . . .the opportunities are unlimited."

That year, with the dream still alive, I entered a contest sponsored by Elsie Robinson, a New York columnist. Her subject to young Americans was, "Whither America." With war clouds hanging over Europe, my essay was titled, "A Stronger Air Force for America." Letters came from the East, the West and even from Nebraska - the Midwest. No offer for Air Corps assignment was received.

In December, 1939, I took my first flying lesson in a Piper Cub airplane. After a few lessons, a friend and I drove to Chicago to purchase a truck for our planned trucking business. A side trip to Harlem Airport on Chicago's south side changed our minds. The "For Sale" sign draped over the propeller of a blue and yellow OX-5 Curtiss Pheasant bi-plane caught my eye. In less than an hour, the owner arrived. A $50.00 down payment was arranged. The license had several months before expiration, so we felt if it made the 90 mile flight to our home in Wisconsin, we would pay the balance of the $175.00 price. At that point, we were willing to fly the "Crate" it came in! The plane was delivered the following Sunday. Our joy was complete!!

That year, 1940, I learned to fly alone as my partner was not able to pass his physical exam required by the Federal Aviation Agency.

That same year, a co-worker, Edmund Janic, suggested we apply for U.S. Army Air Corps Pilot training. That suited me fine! Our High School diplomas required we pass a three-day college test. With some brush up at the University of Wisconsin Extension, Milwaukee, we were able to make it. Janic passed in 1940. I passed in September, 1941.

March 21, 1941, Eddie Janic entered Primary training at Pine Bluffs, Arkansas. His letters were an inspiration to me and I would show them to my fellow construction workers. The "Boss" was also very interested to hear how well Eddie was doing. I kept him informed, I have treasured Eddie's letters and saved every one he sent to me.

Here is what Army Air Corps flying was like in the 1940's, according to Janic:

March 21, 1941

Dear Jackson,

We arrived here a day late due to a stop at Fort Sheridan, but, mister, we're here. James, never in my best pipe dreams did I imagine anything as smooth as this.

We're the first class at this school. It's a brand new one. We have 50 members in the class. We sleep two in a room with private shower, etc. The planes we use are Fairchilds, 175 H.P. PT-19A. They are all brand new, just flown in from the factory. We have twelve now, with ten more due tomorrow.

This place seems more like a health resort than a flying school. The buildings are completely white with red roofs. It looks like a settlement of colonial homes. We march around here in coveralls during the daytime and uniforms at night, glamour style. The uniforms are gray gabardine with an insignia on the left arm and a prop on the cap.

When we got here today they fed us, filled out a form and then marched us right to the barber for Sheik-style hair cuts.

You should see these glamour kids whose curls have withered away to three inches.

Say "hello" to the working men and send me Red's address. Please excuse quality of letter. No time to marshall thoughts. Busier then heck.

Ed.

Address: Flying Cadet, Edmund Janic
Air Corps Training Detachment
Pine Bluffs, Arkansas

To Eddie, I was "Stonewall Jackson" at work, so the nickname "Jackson" was his favorite way of referring to me. His second letter followed a week later and was more on the serious part of the training and the hard work ahead.

It was in April of 1941 that Germany invaded Greece and Yugoslavia and yet there was no break given to high school graduates to become cadets.

The next two letters from Eddie are reprinted here and I can only say that they are a fine explanation of the life of a flying cadet in the early part of the 1940's. Reading these words is like an re-enactment of my Primary cadet days at Ryan School of Aeronautics, in Hemet, California.

"Pine Bluff Arkansas"

"April 2, 1941"

Dear Jackson,

I've changed my opinion about this place being a summer camp. Brother, we're continually on the run.

I fly in the Dawn Patrol, right after breakfast. When I say fly, don't take me too literally. The last couple of days I've been flying like a bird without feathers. I did alright on stalls and spins, but the simple stuff had my number. We fly a rectangular course here. We leave the field and climb to 300 ft., make a 90 degree turn, climb to 500 and then break traffic at a 45 degree angle. The first couple days I had trouble getting orientated, I mean my sense of direction wasn't too good. Now I know my way around and hope I'm improving, but I can't tell you because the instructors tell us nothing.

Glad to hear you got by the physical exam. Take a little advice, study now and don't think I'm kidding. We get eight times as much schooling-regular class work, then we do flying.

About the change of menu, ease your mind on that. It's a shame you can't see the beautiful photograph smiling down at me. And it comes with a southern accent. However, we have very little free time. Saturday afternoons and evenings, and occasionally Sundays are the only liberty periods we have, and half the time we don't leave camp because we have too much homework.

Jackson, keep flying, even though you may get an appointment. These instructors don't treat us as greenies, but expect us to react like veteran pilots. Everything has to be right on the nose or they rake you with hell's fire if you miss.

You tell the company to keep their chins up, you can never tell when I'll be back. Some of the boys have left already. Harry Sewning is here with this detachment. He is a good kid and getting along swell.

I think your Father Ireland is a former professor of mine. Great big guy, swell people, first name is Ray.

It's beginning to look like rain, so imagine we'll have a double dose of ground school tomorrow, oh happy day!

These Fairchilds are dandy airplanes. They have an inline engine, 175 hp. They have a top speed of 135 and cruise about 90. They have a low wing and a rudder as big as a house. They're very stable.

I'm off to the feast of the gods. Here's some parting words.

Study like heck and fly as though your life depended on one degree.

High flying to you,

Eddie"

April 20, 1941

Dear Jim,

I soloed yesterday morning. It was a bigger surprise to me than anyone else. The field is mud from a three-day rain and we flew off a partial field about one-half the size of your airport. The wind was blowing and my instructor was eating my ears off on the ride. When I landed and stopped, he piled out and told me to take it up and fly a rectangular course and land. I darn near fell out of the seat.

I took off and the wind played tricks. I had all I could do to handle it. When I leveled off and made my down-wind turn, I tried to trim it - it was light on the nose, I let the controls go and she picked up 150 feet before you could say ——! I grabbed it and though I'd fly her like that because I was at the place of the base leg turn. You probably guessed it, I overshot. I did the pattern once more and this time I got her trimmed and landed, but right in the middle of a puddle. The goo flew everywhere, including my face. I couldn't see a thing.

I just kept kicking those rudders and praying. It stopped short enough so I taxied back and went up once more and set her down, after a fashion.

We're behind in our flying schedule. That is why we flew

yesterday, Saturday. We were supposed to fly today with no liberty, but the Lord answered our prayers. It rained like heck about 5 o'clock, putting the kibosh on the rest of the field, so the Captain gave us liberty until 7:00 tonight. Maybe you think the Cadets didn't cheer.

An AT-6 from Kelly Field landed here yesterday in all that goo. Is that every a beautiful piece of airplane. This evening when he left, he went around the field wide open and when he passed the ramp he rolled his wings and waved good-bye. He was about 75 feet high and doing about 250 MPH. Beautiful sight!

They've washed out 5 boys in the last couple days. So hold thumbs.

They've expecting a flood stage in this country about the end of the week. Will it ever be a joke if it rises high enough to cover the field. We're about two miles from the Arkansas River and not much higher than it.

Jimmy, with your outlook on glamour girls, this is the place for you. Gee, there are some swell angels in this neck of the woods. I had chow at one's home today. Can she cook, can she sing, has her Daddy got a nice Buick, but so what! We probably won't get to town for some time if the weather is good, until we get caught up with the flying end of this schedule. No visitors allowed on the field, so I guess we'll have to get along without them.

At this juncture please let us devote this limited space to the discussion of ground school. Mister, when that field is bad, we go to school all day, so if you're still planning on this business, study, now. The curriculum of studies moves very rapidly, so if you're prepared beforehand it becomes a little easier.

We're expecting replacements in a week. We're going to be privileged to ride them. It should be fun. But if we're going to ride them, the older class has to be a model. You should see the 20 page typed booklet we received yesterday on behavior and conduct. Penalty for infractions will be marching on the ramp. I can see myself there now... Oh, unhappy day!

I'm supposed to be studying now but I'm taking a chance that if the weather is good we'll fly all day tomorrow and beat them out of ground school.

High flying to you.
Flying Cadet Edmund Janic
Air Corps Training Detachment
Pine Bluff, Arkansas"

This was Eddie's last letter to me from flying school. With his father's health deteriorating, Eddie voluntarily washed out of school to return home and to civilian life to be near his parents in their time of need.

We were again working together on construction jobs. My third try at passing the college requirement test was coming up in September of 1941. I still wanted to be an Army Air Corps pilot. During the week-ends I still accumulated flying time in my OX-5 and even rented other planes with greater horsepower.

The three-day test was given at the University of Chicago and Eddie and I were awaiting the results when the inevitable turn of events changed the lives and destiny of America's youth - the bombing of Pearl Harbor.

Although I was not told by the U.S. Army Corps that I had passed the test taken at the University of Chicago, the Army did send a press release to my home town newspaper, the

Waukesha Daily Freeman that I had passed the test and was on my way to Santa Ana, California for Cadet training. This press release was in the newspaper on February 21, 1942.

Reprint from the Waukesha Daily Freeman

February 21, 1942

IN THE SERVICE

James Bruno, Jr., 23 of Rt. 4, Waukesha, left this morning for cadet training in the U.S. Army Air Corps at Santa Ana, California. A graduate of Waukesha High School, Bruno was interested in civilian flying activities in the Waukesha County Airport. After studying at the University of Wisconsin Extension Division in Milwaukee, he passed his college requirement test in November and was accepted in the Air Corps Tuesday. He is the son of Mr. and Mrs. James Bruno.

My dream of becoming a flying cadet in the U.S. Army Air Corps came true on February 17, 1942 in the form of a telegram through Western Union sent by the Army Recruiting Officer in Milwaukee.

The morning I received my telegram I rushed out to the Waukesha County Airport to show it to my pilot friends gathered there, about a dozen men. Among them were my two flying instructors and a German World War I fighter Ace, Dr. D. H. Bruns. Our U.S. Fighter Ace, Lt. Rodney Williams was not at the field that day. When I happily exhibited my telegram, a friend and pilot, Leonard Pagano asked my instructors if I had a chance of making it in the Air Corps.

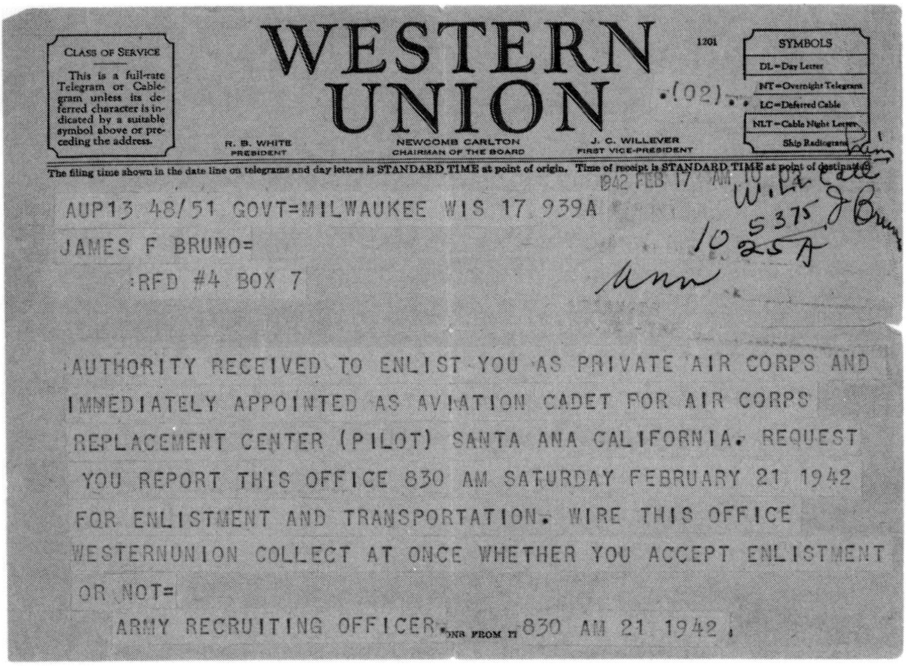

CLASS OF SERVICE
This is a full-rate Telegram or Cablegram unless its deferred character is indicated by a suitable symbol above or preceding the address.

WESTERN UNION

1201

SYMBOLS
DL=Day Letter
NT=Overnight Telegram
LC=Deferred Cable
NLT=Cable Night Letter
Ship Radiogram

R. B. WHITE, PRESIDENT — NEWCOMB CARLTON, CHAIRMAN OF THE BOARD — J. C. WILLEVER, FIRST VICE-PRESIDENT

The filing time shown in the date line on telegrams and day letters is STANDARD TIME at point of origin. Time of receipt is STANDARD TIME at point of destination

1942 FEB 17 AM 10

AUP13 48/51 GOVT=MILWAUKEE WIS 17 939A

JAMES F BRUNO=
:RFD #4 BOX 7

AUTHORITY RECEIVED TO ENLIST YOU AS PRIVATE AIR CORPS AND IMMEDIATELY APPOINTED AS AVIATION CADET FOR AIR CORPS REPLACEMENT CENTER (PILOT) SANTA ANA CALIFORNIA. REQUEST YOU REPORT THIS OFFICE 830 AM SATURDAY FEBRUARY 21 1942 FOR ENLISTMENT AND TRANSPORTATION. WIRE THIS OFFICE WESTERNUNION COLLECT AT ONCE WHETHER YOU ACCEPT ENLISTMENT OR NOT=

ARMY RECRUITING OFFICER. 830 AM 21 1942.

"Jimmy will never make it," said one of the brothers who had soloed me in my own plane one year earlier. "He may make it through Primary training, but will wash out in Basic," he said. The other instructor interrupted and said, "He may get through Basic, but will wash out in Advanced." Upon hearing these remarks, Dr. Bruns came up to me and putting an arm around my shoulder he said, "Don't believe them, Jimmy. You will make an Army pilot, and a good one."

A few days later, Rodney Williams approached me at the airport. Having heard from other people that my instructors said of my chances, he told me, "Don't believe those fools; get in there and show them you will make it."

CHAPTER 2

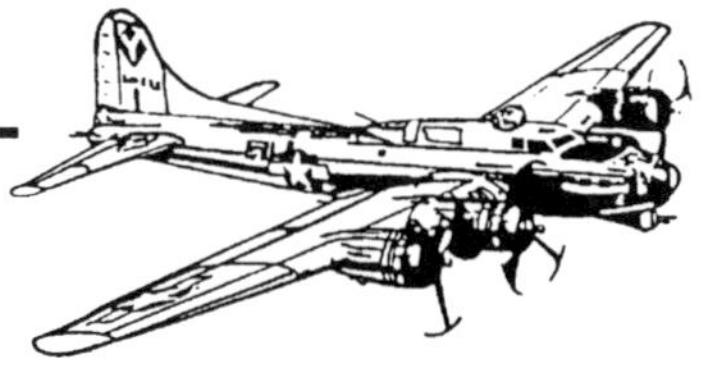

PRIMARY - BASIC - ADVANCED

SILVER WINGS
SEPT. 29, 1942

March 31, 1942 - - - Ryan School of Aeronautics in the beautiful foothills of the San Bernadino Mountains. Our instructors were civilian pilots; our planes, the Ryan P.T.22. Kenneth W. Saupp, a terrific fellow, was my instructor. He took much interest in each of his students and gave them extra help if they needed it. I had six hours and five minutes of dual when he turned me loose for my solo flight. Both ground school classes and the flying came easy to me and by May 14th, received the final Army check ride from Lt. Jensen. Lt. Jensen approved my performance and graduation neared.

Graduation Day! Most of the Cadets wasted no time on weekends in town and had already made plans for the dance. The rest of us were asked if we wanted to arrange a date from the Junior College nearby - what could we say?

The day arrived and a bus load of lovely girls began stepping off the bus. The girls were introduced as they got off and the Cadet's name was called off as the blind dates accepted with smiles. One after another, they appeared lovelier and lovelier. My heart was beating as I anticipated the "dream" date. The last girl came to the door - my heart sank! Why did I get the unattractive one? The rest of the Cadets looked at me and thanked their lucky stars they were not in my shoes.

To the dance we went - but do you think I could trade dances with any of my Cadet pals? As I approached and gave them the eye to change partners, they just grinned and waltzed away. Just wait, fellows, I thought, what comes around, goes around.

We did lose a few Cadets in Primary. Some were high school graduates, others with two to four years of college fell by the wayside. So the Class of 42-1 went on to Basic Training.

BASIC TRAINING - TAFT, CALIFORNIA

Our class arrived at the sandy desert city of Taft on May 28, 1942. Gardner Field was staffed with Army Air Corps instructors. Here, we became familiar with the Vultee BT-13 powered with a 450 horsepower engine. We were to learn instrument flying utilizing the Link Trainer. Basic training included night flying. There were the endless classes to attend; meteorology, navigation, aircraft identification, theory of flight, and others. Lt. Gould was an excellent instructor and was dedicated to making us successful in the course. When the 20 hour check ride came along he was confident there would be no trouble.

The check pilot concluded otherwise. Where I thought I had done a perfect 720 degree turn and struck my own prop wash, he told me it was a stall. There were other maneuvers he didn't like either; the landing was not to his liking. I thought a stall out two feet off the ground wasn't bad at all as the oleo struts absorbed this very well with a minimum of bounce. The check pilot informed me in no uncertain terms that if there wasn't significant improvement by the 40 hour check.. .He didn't have to say the rest.

Lt. Gould was sorry to hear the check ride didn't fare too well; so concentrated on power turns, stalls, landings, and overhead approaches. The 40 hour check ride was given by a different officer. I rated a Captain for this ride and when we got down he was very pleased with my per formance.

Basic Training
Taft, CA., July, 1943

Time to think about the graduation dance. That night I asked Hattie if she would go with me - no more blind dates, remember! Hattie had a brother who worked on the air base as did hundreds of other civilians. One weekend while hitchhiking into town, Homer picked me up and dropped me off at the drive-in stand where Hattie worked. She was just right for the graduation dance - no more kidding about Miss Five-by-Five.

The last phase of our basic training, we had to make a solo-night cross country flight. We went north to Fresno, southwest to Avenal and back to Gardner. We were cautioned that when we got to Fresno and turned southwest, our timing had to be accurate. If we flew three minutes longer, we would be off course and on the ocean side of the coastal range of mountains, known as the Diablo Range. The mountain ranges and the San Joaquin Valley somehow blended into a black carpet at night.

That night we lost our first Aviation Cadet, Richard Farr, one of my close friends. Dick had apparently flown several minutes longer on the southwest leg of the night navigation mission and his error was compounded by a jittery Civil Defense unit on the west coast. A blackout was ordered as they heard the drone of the BT-13. Richard groped helplessly along the California coast to find an airport to make an EMERGENCY landing since he had crossed the mountains. But there was no relief and he flew out over the Pacific with his gas supply running low. He refused to bail out over the populated coast and endanger the lives of those below.

Those who had mistaken him for an enemy bomber could never know the sick feeling when he saw all landmark lights go out on him at a time when he needed them most. We learned his parachute was found washed up on the beach several weeks later. Richard became the first casualty of the Class of 42-1. "When the last flight is over, and we meet the Flying Boss, you will know the air will be filled again, from Arion to the Cross." These last lines of the song we sang in Primary surely apply to Richard.

"I'VE GOT BELLS THAT JINGLE JANGLE JINGLE"

This was the title of one of our popular songs during the year 1942. One morning my flight instructor, a young second lieutenant, came to work late, singing that tune. He was badly in need of a shave and, undoubtedly, some sleep. The flight instructors shook their heads as they observed him in that condition and we, the students, had hoped he would send us up to get some solo time while he took the morning off. It must have been some party! He was still flying high as he told us that he was taking us up to show us how to spin the BT-13! Well, we almost fell out of our parachutes! "Bruno," he said, "You will go first." Relief flooded the faces of the other four students! But I was game, no matter how dangerous the maneuver would be. We were told the spin would, at times, get violent and we would lose considerable altitude before recovery.

I was instructed to climb to an altitude of 7,500 feet and level off. We cleared the area to make sure there were no other planes in our vicinity or below us. My instructor said very little as we climbed over the desert sands around Taft on that bright sunny day. I made up my mind that if the plane was not brought out of the spin in the one and one-half turns that he said we would do, I would take over. After all, I had a good night's sleep and had a clear head, so why worry?

The time for the demonstration finally arrived as my instructor took over the controls. He told me he would spin the plane and recover in one and one-half turns. He headed the plane to the east and reduced the power as he slowly brought the nose up to a stalling attitude. The plane went into a violent spin as he kicked the full left rudder. I knew when we completed the first turn, he would have to act quickly to stop the spin in the next half turn. We were coming around to the west when I decided it was time for action. I popped the stick forward, then kicked full right rudder as the plane stopped at two turns with the altimeter still crazily unwinding. I eased back on the stick to reduce the excessive air speed and leveled off just below 5,000 feet. "You see what I mean," my instructors said, "we lost 2,500 feet in that spin." With that, he proposed we head back to the field. Little did he realize he was not the pilot who brought the plane out of the spin, but I let him think so!

The carefree days at Taft were coming to a close; the date for the graduation dance was announced. This time I was prepared ... there would be no blind date, or would there? Bob Imrie had his eye on Hattie and asked her before I had a chance.

Hattie was kind to arrange a date for me. Miss Burnes could have passed for a Hollywood starlet so I didn't mind the change of events one bit. Long after graduation and while in combat training I wrote to Miss Burnes and her wonderful parents.

ON TO ADVANCED

July 30, 1942 we participated in twin engine training in Roswell, New Mexico. In our first two weeks we flew the wonderful AT-6 single engine trainer. It was a great thrill to fly with its retractable landing gear and constant speed propeller.

Flying the twin engine Cessna did not compare with the power and maneuverability of the AT-6. But we needed multi-engine training and the "bamboo bomber," as the AT-17 Cessna was commonly referred to, was to prepare Second Lieutenants.

My first night flight in the Cessna was a disaster. My instructor and I survived a near mid air collision inside a cloud bank but didn't do too well as we came in for the landing. When the weather played games that night, all planes in the air were called in to land as the field was closing. My instructor took over the controls for the landing.

In the clouds we saw a plane go past in the opposite direction as we made our way around the field to the downwind leg. The student and instructor were probably looking for a break in the overcast to spot the field lights below. Over the radio, there was a constant flow of instructions to the planes that had located the field and information on the position of the other planes. We were about the third in line to land and I put the wheel switch in the "down" position on the final approach. We had broken out of the overcast on our downwind leg and, frankly, both of us were quite shaken up from the sight of that plane whizzing past us in the overcast.

The wheels slowly ground down and the autosyn indicator dial showed both wheels to be down. We were descending "power on" in our landing approach. A few seconds before touch down with the "power off," the warning horn suddenly began to sound!

My instructor looked puzzled and before he could react, the wheels touched the runway and next the propellers began hitting the concrete. The wheels had not locked down and as my instructor applied full power for a quick take-off, I shouted over the sudden roar of the splintered propellers, "Cut the power, we just ground off the props!"

I quickly pulled the emergency release as the exit door flew off. The tower sensed something was wrong as the squadron commander's voice came over the radio and confirmed that we were totally disabled three-fourths of the way down the active runway.

The following day the investigation of the plane's landing gear provided the answer. The limit switch was defective. Both my instructor and I were absolved of any responsibility for the accident.

My other harrowing experience also occurred on a night training flight. I was in the left seat and my cadet partner was flying co-pilot. We had been warned that lights on the ground could disorient us and appear to be the lights of another plane in the distance. I was on the final approach to shoot a landing when we both saw what we thought was another plane making a base leg to our right and at our flight level of 1,000 feet. I told Cadet Keegan that I would lower the nose to get below the other ship. We kept seeing the light to our right and I kept pushing the nose into a steeper dive. Suddenly, Keegan called out, "Pull up, Bruno, pull up! I can see the daisies!" And the light we were avoiding? It was a red light on the ground about half a mile to our right! Somehow, I wasn't thinking so much of myself but Cadet Keegan was married. I almost made his wife a widow!

At advanced flying there were very few men who washed out, although the possibility was ever present, up to the last few weeks of the course. My classroom grades proved satisfactory. I was looking forward to the final graduation and the gold bars of a second lieutenant.

I didn't have to look for a date this time. Back in Primary I had already told my fiance, Irene, that she had to come to my graduation when and if I got my wings. When my cadet friend, Ray Reid, found out my fiance was coming to Roswell, he suggested we have a double wedding. He had met a girl in Roswell whose father had a Packard auto and, until he mentioned the wedding, I was sure the only thing he was in love with was the Packard!

When Irene arrived she didn't know that Ray and I had planned the double wedding. We had been engaged over eight months and the night she arrived I asked her to be my wife. I was a happy cadet when she said, "Yes!" I told Cadet Reid the next day that the wedding was "on." But Ray by this time had chickened out! In the few days left before graduation, we went to a Catholic priest in town to arrange the wedding for September 30, 1942. The priest refused to marry a Catholic and a Lutheran without a thirty day instruction course. We told him we were leaving Roswell on September 30th and didn't have the time for the course.

"THE FIRST ECUMENICAL WEDDING" TAKES PLACE

I returned to the base and told my cadet friend, Hal Gunn, my problem. "Tell you what," he said. "Gerry and I were married last week by the base chaplain. All four of us will go and call on Chaplain Brinberry and we can stand up for you."

The Chaplain agreed and plans were made for the wedding on September 30th.

First came the graduation of September 29th and the Class of "42-1" proudly received their wings.

We had received three choices of assignment and Hal suggested we take bomber training in Salt Lake City. That way he could be closer to home. So I agreed with him. The other two choices were photo reconnaissance at Denver, where we would have been assigned to P-38's or the ferry command, which would have sent us to Long Beach, California.

I still wonder to this day... .what made us want to go into combat anyway?

Now, back to the wedding! The next morning I was at the altar, a Catholic marrying a Lutheran, the service being conducted by a Protestant Chaplain, and our best man and matron were Mormons. I'm sure we must have initiated the Ecumenical Movement that day in 1942!

Our orders were cut and directed Hal and me, among others, to report to Salt Lake City. We packed after the wedding and set off, traveling all night, with our wives changing off driving. Hal's car led the way and we followed him. We arrived about 9:30 the next morning and after meeting Hal's parents and his brother, we proceeded to locate housing, which turned out to be futile. That night Hal's brother offered the hospitality of the room they had suggested we take on our arrival, as they warned us the hotels and motels were filled. The next day we reported to our station only to find we were given another change of station and had to proceed to Gowen Field, Boise, Idaho. Again, we packed and proceeded to Boise.

Upon checking in at the Air Base we inquired about housing off base and were given the address of a basement apartment another officer and his wife had vacated. We were agreed we could rent the two bedroom apartment. To date we have remained constant friends of the Pipal's and have exchanged greetings each Christmas for the past fifty years. Boise was one city where the service man was welcomed and made to feel a part of the community.

Ryan School of Aeronautics Graduation
May, 1942

CHAPTER 3

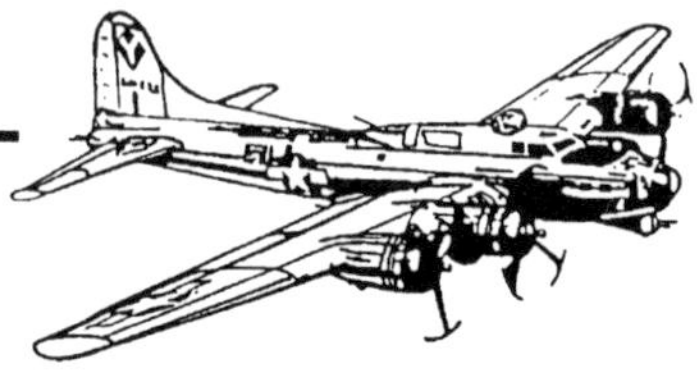

B-17 Training And Overseas Deployment

The month of October, 1943, thirty-six members of the graduating Class of 42-1 at Boise, Idaho, a bomber training base, were performing well enough to fly the first pilot seat.

October 31, we were informed training for first pilots was suspended and combat crews were formed. We went to combat as co-pilots and obtained first pilot experience in the months ahead. Our first pilots had already trained for over three months and they were ready for overseas transition.

Our B-17 instructor, Captain Harry Burrell, selected me for his co-pilot in combat and had already selected a very skillful navigator, Joe Boyle, and a top bombardier, David Fronefield. The gunners were enlisted men and in the top of their class. All of us were in our 20's with the exception of tail gunner, Jack Guerard, who was 35 years old.

Our next move was to Walla Walla, Washington. We believe the reason for moving was to get acclimated to cold weather and mountains.

David's and my wife were with us and found a charming Tudor style home to rent. Captain Burrell and Joe Boyle stayed at the Bachelor Officer Quarters. That happy balance readily changed one morning.

Joe reported for flying and told Captain Burrell he had called his fiance, Paula, who lived in Sacramento, California and proposed marriage over the telephone. He asked her to get on the next train so they could get married on her arrival.

My wife, Irene, Joe and I made wedding arrangements with the Catholic church. Irene and I were their attendants. Now, Harry was left as the one bachelor among the officers of the crew.

On September 16, we cleared the base and headed for Sioux City, Iowa. Our wives were forced to make the wintry trip by car though the mountains! Their trip was a harrowing experience. The fog steadily thickened as they drove on a mountain road. To continue moving through, they were obliged to get out of the car to read the road sign and helplessly watched their automobile slide off the icy road and into the ditch. Somehow, they made it to Sioux City much to the relief of their very concerned husbands!

Our flying trip was also difficult, with bad weather. Captain Burrell, as usual, was checking out a first pilot who was one of several on board. This pilot had transferred to us from the Royal Canadian Air Force.

We were caught in a severe snowstorm over the State of Wyoming. Captain Burrell decided to climb to eleven thousand feet to give us several thousand feet of clearance over the mountains. After an hour at eleven thousand, the pilot felt we were clear of the mountains and decided it was time to descend. Harry did not agree with him and suggested continued flying at eleven thousand. The First Lieutenant persisted and Captain Burrell finally relented to a slow descent.

The blizzard continued unabated. Navigator Joe was no help as he was under the impression we were flying by radio navigation. Everyone on board was concerned and peering out the windows for some visible break in the swirling snowstorm. Suddenly, an open space in the driving snow revealed we were encountering jagged mountain peaks ahead! We had not passed Cheyenne, Wyoming as the pilot wanted to believe. Power was immediately applied to all four engines and we climbed to a safe altitude, all sighing a breath of relief.

The pilot who almost crashed our plane into the mountains was reassigned to an Air Sea Rescue group. There is no room for error when the lives of ten men are at risk.

Our training at the Sioux City Air Base concentrated on formation flying, night navigation, aerial gunnery, practice bombing and rendezvous with other aircraft. This was to be our final training base prior to picking up the B-17-F's, our combat planes. We worked together as a combat team and learned to know our respective jobs better. We were taught about the bombsight operation. All crewmen became familiar with the operation of the fifty caliber machine guns and both turrets.

Each man was proficient in his job so that no man, by omission of his required duty would endanger the entire crew.

One night, Bankhead and I were scheduled to meet another plane at ten thousand feet over Sioux City. Bankhead gave the controls to me while in a banking turn and said he wanted to make sure I kept my eye on the lights of Sioux City. At ten thousand feet, we could see the City of Omaha, Nebraska 64 miles to the south. I was still in a banking turn when he returned to his seat. Looking down from that altitude he asked, "Where is Sioux City?" My hesitation was all

Bankhead needed. Back at the controls he said, "You're usually wrong," and headed for the lights of Omaha.

Over our radio we could hear the other plane had reached Sioux City at the appointed time and here we were, over Omaha. By the time Bankhead discovered my guess was correct, the other plane gave up on us and landed. We sheepishly told the other crew of our disorientation while circling.

By the end of December, 1943, our training was completed and all crews were given a ten-days leave before our final overseas preparation.

Irene and I had a day's drive to my home in Waukesha. We enjoyed a pleasant visit with our family and neighbors. We visited Dr. Bruns in Milwaukee and I introduced him to my new bride. Pleasantries were exchanged and he was happy to know I "made the grade" and earned the silver wings. As we were leaving his office, he said, "Jimmy, we are making a terrible mistake! The Germans are a fine people and they are a great nation." I did not reply as we shook hands and said good-bye. My wife and I discussed the remark and dismissed it as a normal statement for a German to make.

After my leave, I said good-bye to my wife and family and returned to Sioux City by train. In a few days, we traveled to Salina, Kansas by troop train.

At the Salina Air Base, we witnessed acres and acres of B-17's and B-24's, fresh from the factories. The weather was cold; down to zero and blowing snow. There was a flurry of activity as crews were picking up supplies needed for the overseas trip. No one knew our destination.

On the night we arrived at Salina, many crews had completed their processing and planes were already departing the base. The planes taxiing out were B-24 Liberators. We watched the formation taxi out. The first plane off began to retract its wheels and was soon followed by the take-off run of the second plane. We heard it lose power several hundred feet off the ground. It plunged to earth and exploded in flames! We could see the third ship of the first flight was airborne and continuing on schedule. That squadron lost their first crew on the eve of their overseas departure leg. We knew their feelings, losing those who had trained with them, as we had experienced the loss one month earlier in Sioux City, Iowa.

The weather that night was near zero and those open plains may have been ideal for unobstructed flying terrain. But no thanks. We cared very little for those raw wintry winds as they cut right through our flying jackets.

The 99th finally checked out all of their B-17-F's and on January 23, 1943, we left for the warmer temperatures of De Ridder, Louisiana. We loved that wonderful 65 degree weather.

The next day we flew an eleven hour overwater mission which would take us over the Gulf of Mexico to Tampa, Florida and return on a non-stop flight. Our departure time was five hours before sundown. As darkness set in, I prayed those engines would keep operating smoothly and get us safely back. The prospect of ditching at night did go through my mind. We had a moonlit night and were happy when Joe called the Tampa tower to advise we were over their station and returning to our base in Louisiana.

As we approached the coast, we found a front had moved in and we were required to let down through the overcast to locate the De Ridder Air Base. After letting down to one thousand feet, ground fog obscured the base, including the terrain for miles around. We criss-crossed the area in vain but there was no sight of the landing field. It was getting close to midnight and our fuel supply was dwindling. We could hear much conversation over the radio and soon caught a message directing us to proceed to the Shreveport Air Base. This was a welcome message as we headed north away from the foggy coast. After overnight billeting, we were able to return to De Ridder the following day.

January 31st we left De Ridder for the palm trees and balmy breezes of Homestead, Florida where we spent several days preparing for the first leg of the overseas trip.

The morning of February 4th we headed for Borinquen Field, on the island of Puerto Rico. It was a six hour and forty minute flight but somehow, about one hour after leaving the Florida coast, our plane's number three engine began running rough; so we feathered the engine and continued on with the other three engines to destination. The next day the mechanics made the needed repair and we took a two and one-half hour test flight to make sure all was well.

Atkinson Field, on the South American coast was our next stop. We took off early on the morning of February 7th and landed at the British Guiana base for an overnight stop. Here we were introduced to tents and mosquito nets for the first time. Sleeping in the 90 degree humid jungle weather was not the hospitality we expected. The next morning we were happy to leave for the twelve hundred mile flight to the Belem airport situated on the south bank of the Amazon River.

A few hundred miles after take-off we ran into heavy rain and storm clouds at our cruising level. The Colonel briefed all pilots to break formation at five minute intervals and fly to our next destination alone. Two planes collided in the storm. It wasn't long before we heard Lt. Moseley's voice transmission - "Hey, there's a plane flying without a tail!" The wing had sheared off the rudder and tail fin of the crippled plane. But all went well and both pilots skillfully brought each plane safely to destination.

We witnessed a continuous cloud burst over the Amazon. It was a hundred miles wide at the mouth and there were times we were certain we were swimming ten feet under the river. However, the altimeter displayed an altitude of 500 feet above sea level. When we were over a large grassy island we were relieved. The briefing officer had told us this was halfway across the Amazon. Upon reaching the south bank of the Amazon we spent an anxious twenty minutes before locating the Belem Airport.

The morning of February 9th we flew to Natal, Brazil. This city was on the easternmost tip of the province, or on the "lion's nose." This point in the country of South America would position us at the shortest distance to the coast of Africa. Two days rest was taken here as we prepared for the eleven hour trip across the Atlantic Ocean. To get to the coast of Africa and the Bathurst landing strip on the Gold Coast was going to test Joe, our navigator. There would be no sleep on this flight.

Our group was briefed for the take-off for ten o'clock, the evening of February 11th. The planes would depart separately, at ten minute intervals, and proceed alone. All crews were instructed to get plenty of sleep in preparation of the overnight flight.

We started out with a clear moonlit night and about halfway across the Atlantic, flying at ten thousand feet we ran into a storm with severe lightning. It was an eerie feeling as the storm lasted for over an hour. The thought of being struck by lightning was ever present. The thought of being in life rafts in the middle of the Atlantic, night or day, was not good.

With the first rays of morning light, we were still three hours from the coast of Africa. Joe had tirelessly guided us "on course" all night. He shot the stars with his sextant when the clouds permitted and used the plotter at times the stars were obscured. When the estimated time of arrival had come, we were at some ten thousand feet and the coast was thick with haze. Joe told us we were over Cape St. Mary and to let down through the haze and the airport steel mat would be five miles inland at the edge of the jungle. We never for one moment doubted Joe's word. We broke out of the thick African haze at an altitude of less than two thousand feet and, sure enough, the steel landing mat was immediately visible. Our Deputy Commander had just landed ahead of us and could not taxi back until we had completed our landing.

For months after sweating out a long flight, Bankhead would ask me to unlock his side window latch. It was easier for the co-pilot to unlock and was also his duty. I misunderstood his command and as we were approximately halfway down the short landing strip, I unlocked the tail wheel instead. The swiveling tail wheel caused the plane to zig-zag toward the waiting B-17 of our Deputy Commander.

A bewildered Bankhead jumped on the brakes as the Deputy Commander braced for us to crash into his waiting plane. After we both taxied back to the parking area, the Deputy Commander, Lt. Col. Le Roy Rainey, wanted an explanation. He admonished me for over three minutes and my ears burned for the next half hour. This would be the first time my ears were to play tricks on me.

The British had jungle accommodations ready for us. Tents and mosquito netting. No air conditioning. The steaming jungles are just that! Steaming jungles! The British were acclimated to that mode of living but it was difficult for us to adjust.

The next day, February 12, we crossed the endless waste of the Sahara Desert. To our surprise, we did see occasional camel caravans. The majestic Atlas Mountains rose above the northern edge of the Sahara. They appeared to be more formidable than the desert. The mountains were snow capped, reminding us of our Rockies back home. It was a welcome relief to reach the plateau of the Moroccan resort town of Marrakesh. It was like Texas - well, almost!

This resort area was fit for Kings and Sheiks. The Hotel de La Mammounia was plush. The Arab elite sure knew how to live. I was glad Uncle Sam was footing the hotel tab. We paid for our meals. Breakfast was twenty-five cents and, for fifty cents, our noon meal was a feast. Our two weeks here was like a carefree vacation in a strange land. We visited the city and were given tours of the surrounding palaces and other buildings with rich mosaic walls and arches. Only in history books had we seen this architecture before. We soon learned; however, we did not come to Africa for a vacation.

CHAPTER 4

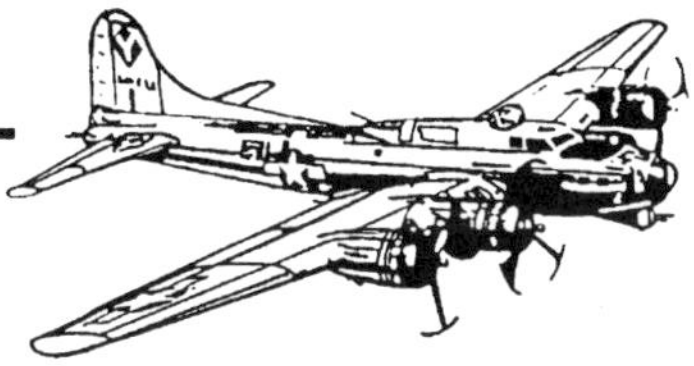

THE ORAN TRAINING BASE

On March 5, 1943, we left the resort city of Marrakesh and the fine accommodations of the Hotel de La Mammounia. Our next stop was the French Air Base at Oran in French Morocco. We were housed in barracks, reminiscent of the French Foreign Legion, with the parade grounds occupying the center of the complex. We also saw many U.S. Army tents set up around the grounds.

By March 27th, 1943, we had practiced our gunnery, high altitude missions, formation, navigation and practice bombing missions. We prepared to leave Oran. During our stay we accumulated a variety of extra supplies and equipment which we loaded into the plane. Among the goods was a French bicycle and a good sized load of lumber for flooring to use in our tent. When I had to get out of bed, I wanted to set foot on dry lumber, not cold African mud.

By the time we had our plane packed for departure, the baggage compartment looked like a gypsy bus. All the spare aircraft supplies stored in the plane were buried with our "comforts of home"!! The lumber was stretched all the way to the tail compartment and I kept assuring "Banky" we should be able to get off the ground somehow, even if we had to pray a little.

That afternoon Captain Burrell stopped by to check on each of his planes. You should have seen the expression on his face when he looked into the tail door of our plane! He walked over to "Banky" to discuss the weight and balance. "Go talk to Jim," "Banky" told him. The Captain came to me and asked if I had used the slide rule and checked the weight and balance. I didn't tell him my slide rule was buried beneath the maze of excess property we had accumulated, but assured him we had calculated the plane should get off in the 5,000 feet of runway.

I guess I wasn't too convincing. The next morning, after a worry filled night, the Captain showed up at our plane and said to us, "I think I would feel better if I flew your plane off this field." We had no objection and I moved out of the co-pilot seat and Bankhead took my place. It would take all the skill a pilot had to get this plane off and we all knew it.

The Captain warmed up the engines and began to taxi out for take-off. We watched the other planes gracefully leave the ground with thousands of feet of runway to spare. Finally, we were in position on the runway. The Captain held the brakes and advanced the throttles. We were almost at full power as he released the brakes and the plane began its roll down the runway. Bankhead called off the air speed as it slowly built up, but the runway was fast disappearing behind us.

We had used up over half the runway and the tail wheel was still on the ground. In the nose compartment, Joe was worrying about the trees at the end of the runway as they loomed larger every second. Behind the co-pilot seat, I nervously watched the air speed needle slowly move toward the 100 miles per hour. We would need at least 110 to get our heavy load off the ground. There was no aborting the take-off now, we would have to get off and clear those trees or else! I glanced at the Captain's face. He was trying hard to pull the plane into the air. It seemed an eternity before it became airborne as we passed a few feet above the trees - - - all of us were scared to hell!

We began to breathe normally again and were glad that ordeal was over.

OUR FIRST BOMBING MISSION

The group moved from the base at St. Donat near Oran to Navarin, a town about one-hundred-twenty miles southwest of Oran. This was on March 27th, three weeks after our arrival in Oran. The Air Base had just been completed for our use, the advance party being there some two weeks prior to our arrival.

We lost no time getting the tents set up and preparing trenches and fox holes. The fox holes were delayed by most of the men as they felt the ground was too dry and rocky. Besides, we were well behind the lines for the enemy to bother us. However, I well remember one night when enemy bombers did appear overhead, and there was no place to hide from the impending attack for those who had not dug their fox hole. I must admit that I was among the ones who had scoffed at digging. It is the most helpless feeling to know that bombs will be exploding near you and there is no quick way to get below ground level. Joe recalled, the next day, that several men jumped right into the slit trenches in self preservation.

On the afternoon of March 30th, we were advised of our first bombing mission. All crewmen pitched in to refuel the planes out of five gallon cans as the refueling trucks had not yet arrived. This took most of the afternoon since delivery from the fuel dump was delayed through lack of suitable trucks to deliver the five gallon cans to the planes.

Lt. Bruno, Co-pilot
Lt. Fronefield, Bombardier

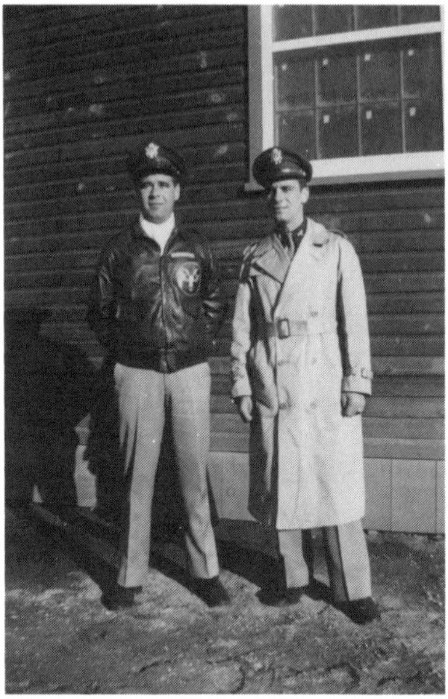

Lt. Boyle, Navigator;
Lt. Bruno, Co-pilot

Left to right: Lt. H.B. Bankhead, S/Sgt. Frank Kovac, 2nd. Lt. James F. Bruno, 2nd. Lt. David L. Fronefield, T/Sgt. James J. Florek

The Ordnance crews began delivering the bombs throughout the afternoon and it was near evening before we began loading them into the bomb bay racks. With numerous other details to ready the planes for the mission, it was after midnight when most of the ground crew and flight crews got to bed for much needed rest.

Five-thirty came around all too soon as the weary men tumbled out of bed and made their way to the mess line in the darkness. No one complained about the lack of sleep or of being tired. We were keyed up for the chance to get on with the first mission.

Once inside the briefing tent, our Group Commander, Colonel Upthegrove, asked if any crews were too tired to go on the day's mission. He got a unanimous "NO!" from the assembled crews. He thanked the men for the long and hard hours they had put in and for their enthusiasm on this, their first mission.

The day's mission was carefully planned with our group staff and that of the veteran 98th Bomb Group Staff. The 98th was to strike another target fifteen minutes ahead of us. They would draw the enemy fighters away from our target area which was the Villacidro Airdrome. We would then go in and drop fragmentation bombs onto the Air Base where the fighters had just left. The round trip was estimated at four hours and since no enemy fighter opposition was expected, we did not have any escort of our own. The Villacidro Airdrome is in Southern Sardinia near the eastern coast. The weather was clear and the flight across the Mediterranean was a sight to remember. From sixteen thousand feet the countryside around the island of Sardinia was peaceful. The mountains rose majestically a short distance from the coast as if guarding the beautiful valleys below.

Colonel Upthegrove, leading the group, reached the initial point and turned down the bomb run. We had not been challenged by a single enemy plane. Anti-aircraft fire tried to reach our altitude, but fell hundreds of feet short. It was an exhilarating feeling to turn off the target and see the buildings on the Airdrome below set on fire from well placed bombs. The men of the 98th knew their strategy as the mission went off as planned.

On the Group's second mission, we were scheduled as a spare plane and were to accompany the group formation to the Mediterranean Coast. Should any of the twenty-four ships in the formation have to drop out due to any engine difficulty or other valid reason, we would slip into that spot in the formation and proceed on to the target. However, on this date, April 15th, we returned as none of the planes had operational problems.

On April 10th, we attacked the Italian Naval Base at LA Maddalene, in Sicily. The planes carried 500 pound demolition bombs and we did an excellent job of covering the target area. The following day we struck the harbor and Naval facilities at Marsala, Sicily with little opposition.

There seemed to be no end to good targets to strike this early in the campaign. The following day our target was the Airdrome at Trapani, Sicily. Here we met the first real opposition from enemy fighters. They were trying to protect their runways from being damaged and the hangar and shops from destruction. Their efforts, however, proved in vain as we covered the target and returned home safely.

After that mission the crew rested for five days. This was done so all crews would not complete their 50 combat missions at one time and the replacement crews would have experienced pilots to lead the squadrons or flight.

CHAPTER 5

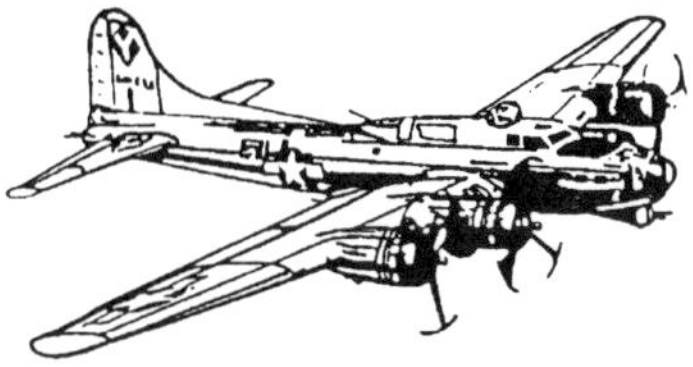

Bizerte, Palermo, Civitavechia Harbor

BIZERTE, TUNIS MISSION
3RD MAY, 1943

On the 3rd of May, 1943, there was excitement on the base. We received word the Germans had assembled a large number of concrete barges to ferry equipment and supplies from the African coast to the island of Sicily. They were desperately trying to keep these supplies from falling into Allied hands. They knew their days in North Africa were numbered.

The decision to go on the mission was continually delayed for updated reconnaissance reports. Finally, in the middle of the afternoon, the mission was "ON". Two bomb groups, ours and a new one just arrived from the States, the 101st Bomb Group, were to participate. They took off and began to assemble for the two hour and fifty minute round trip as dusk was setting in. The weather worsened during the afternoon and we had overcast skies. Bankhead and I flew 45 minutes when the No. 3 engine began to overheat. All efforts to bring the cylinder head temperature down were in vain. We were forced to shut down the engine, leave the formation and return to base. After we landed and taxied to our parking stand, night was setting in. "How can the other 47 planes find their way back to their field without lights and no navigation aids?", we asked each other.

That night we were to lose eight of our B-17's to weather, without dropping a single bomb on the enemy. Here is the press release of the 50th mission, the night of May 3, 1943.

TWENTY PLANES TAKE OFF TO BOMB BIZERTE, THREE RETURN TO BASE.

"Then, there was that memorable night of May 3rd when only three airplanes reached their home base after a bombing mission to Bizerte."

"Weather, the implacable enemy of all flying men, scattered the group like a hawk after a flock of chickens. Men parachuted to earth, crash landings were made in the sea and in the mountains. One crew was forced to land with a full load of bombs with an engine on fire. They managed to get out of the plane and dashed about 200 yards behind a sand dune when the bombs let loose. They escaped unhurt. Seven men were lost in the sea in the anxious two days that followed. Many were the tales of dogged determination to save airplanes and crews; the bravery of these American lads as they wended their way down precipitous mountain sides on mules and on camels as they cracked the silk in the darkness."

Our Colonel was among the ones able to find their way to home base in that night overcast. There was no way to identify the base in the clouds as they returned. Our deputy commander radioed a British warship in the Mediterranean off Cape Bone, as they ditched in the darkness. They were not picked up as planned, and only one life raft inflated for the ten men. They had to hang over the side with their bodies dangling in the frigid sea. After a period of time, they became delirious and in agony. Four men slipped into the water and were lost. The deputy commander, his co-pilot, the bombardier and three gunners survived after drifting to a rocky reef near the shoreline.

Captain McLaughlin was unable to find the field in the darkness. Knowing that under the overcast were jagged mountains, gullies and lakes, he and his crew successfully bailed out, as did Captain Davis and his crew. Captain Burrell found a small base for B-25's and touched down on the short runway, only to have his landing gear fail and skid the plane on its belly, over the end of the runway.

Captain Mosely's plane landed wheels-up in the middle of a dry lake, and slid atop wet clay for more than a thousand yards. One plane crash-landed in a river bed. The men scrambled to safety just before all their bombs exploded. The remaining two planes landed at fighter bases and were damaged after skidding off the ends of the shorter runways. Men made their way back to the base from every point on the compass over the next few days as we anxiously waited for them to return unharmed.

Our group had ten missions to its credit. Our crew had gone on six of them. Ironically, the 301st Bomb Group, also on this mission, was able to find their way back to their base in the darkness of Africa. The 301st had followed the 97th Bomb Group to England early in the war, had flown a few missions out of England and flew to Africa in November, 1942. Our group had arrived from the States in February, 1943. You can bet that our navigators were furnished maps giving the location of all bases in our North African operations area.

It would only be speculation as to what the fate of our crew would have been. Our navigator, who guided us across the Atlantic to Africa for a perfect landfall had the habit of telling us to "follow the leader" whenever we asked our position. It had first happened to us over Brazil when our group ran into a severe storm near the Amazon jungle. The colonel told the planes to break formation and peel off in five minute intervals and fly through the storm alone. We were at an altitude of less than 6,000 feet when we asked Joe our position. He awoke and said, "How the hell do I know? Just follow the leader!" It did not take him too long to determine the distance from the take-off from British Guiana and the elapsed time on our southerly heading. We were soon flying across the mouth of the Amazon, over a one hundred mile expanse of muddy water. We had no problem finding Belem, our next destination.

Without Joe and his Irish humor, ours would have been a very serious crew. Many a time he would return from a visit to a nearby town in Africa, go to the chaplain and tell him he had located the local bar, and suggest they both go there for a drink.

(Author's note:) After his 50th mission and return to the States, we lost track of Joe. After the 99th Bomb Group Historical Society was formed some ten years ago, George Coen, one of the founders, kept writing me to find Joe. Finally, a few years ago, we contacted the Medical Society in Boston and discovered Joe had gone on to become a doctor. He had recently passed away. We remember Joe for his love of life.

MOTHER'S DAY
MAY 9 1943

This was one morning that we did not have our hearts in going out on a bombing mission. There were two reasons — it was Mother's Day and we knew the photo reconnaissance planes had just confirmed the City of Palermo was bristling with anti-aircraft guns; scattered, alert and constantly dangerous.

The High Command decided we would fly over the harbor without bombing it, then hover over and around the city to knock out as many anti-aircraft as we could. This would make it easier for us to come back here again and again. We knew, however, in the future one well-timed shot would bring down our plane. We could hardly expect to knock out all of those belching guns in today's raid.

Intelligence reports revealed the residents of Palermo were so comfortable with us and so sure of our precision bombing of the ships in their harbor that when the sirens sounded the citizens would gather at vantage points on the roofs of downtown buildings and watch us try our best for destructive hits, of which we'd had our share. Wars are made up of tricky surprises. We skimmed over the harbor and opened our bomb bay doors. We were over the city itself! There was heavy anti-aircraft fire, naturally, and the fighters came up in waves to beat us off. But damage to the city guns had been done.

One B-17 did go down, although it appeared to us as the men got out safely before the plane spun out of control. Their safety might have come to an abrupt end. You can surmise what happened when that crew touched down and came face to face with the angry people of Palermo. (The story of their capture and ordeal is related in Chapter 7.)

This particular mission was extremely discomforting to me and I sensed the other men on my plane were equally uneasy about it. Importantly, it was another mission credited to our

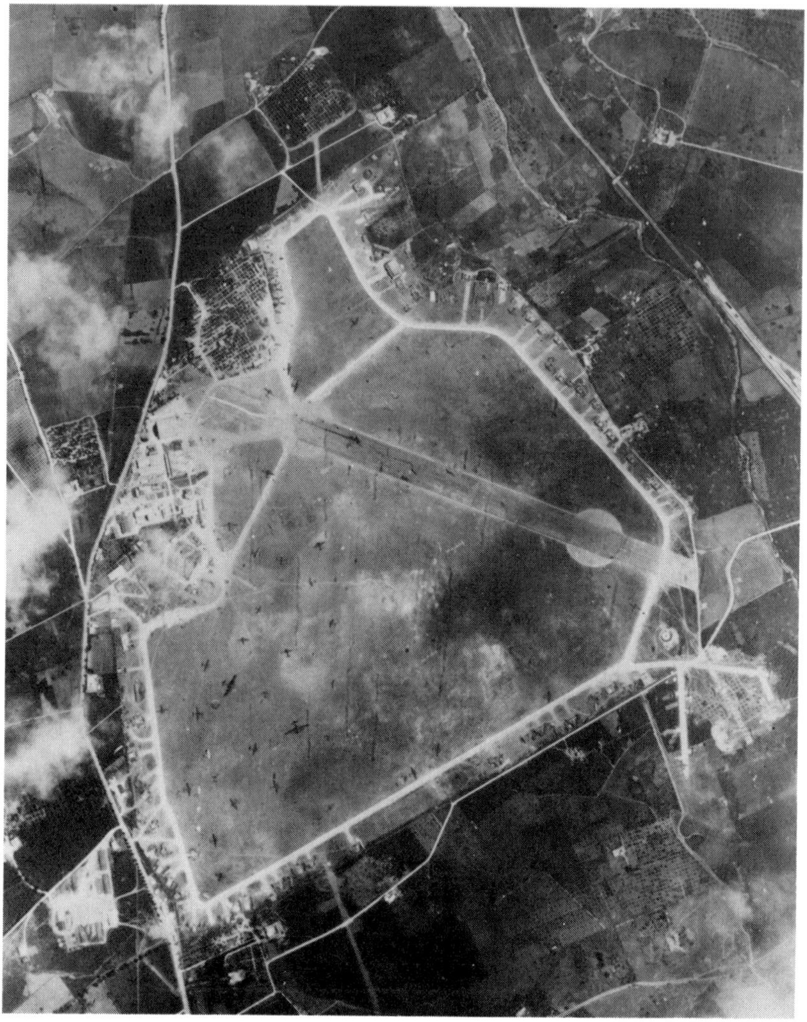

Photo: Courtesy Gen. Upthegrove

MILO AIRDROME, SICILY

Photo shows pinpoint saturation bombing carried out May 10, 1943. The airdrome had 122 Axis aircraft, including 60 Single engine fighters, 29 Medium Bombers and 33 Transports.

An important phase of the Allied Strategic plan was to knock out enemy landing fields.

The field was almost completely blanketed by bomb bursts, rendering it useless and destroying or severely damaging nearly all of the enemy aircraft present when the attack began.

The 99th Bomb Group was awarded the PRESIDENTIAL UNIT CITATION after this mission account. One by one, the total mounted in the book and I was still alive! Chalk up Mission No. 8 for our crew.

TARGET CIVITAVECHIS HARBOR
MAY 14, 1943

This mission took us up the northern coast of Italy and covered seven hours and twenty minutes flying time. The weather was clear and we could plainly see dozens of ships riding at anchor in the harbor below. Our photographs showed we destroyed sixteen ships. The railroad yards were also hit by part of the same formation. Anti-aircraft fire was very light and no fighters rose to challenge the formation. This coastal area was quite mountainous and fighters would have to come fifty to one hundred miles inland if they were to intercept us. This was mission number 12 for me.

CHAPTER 6

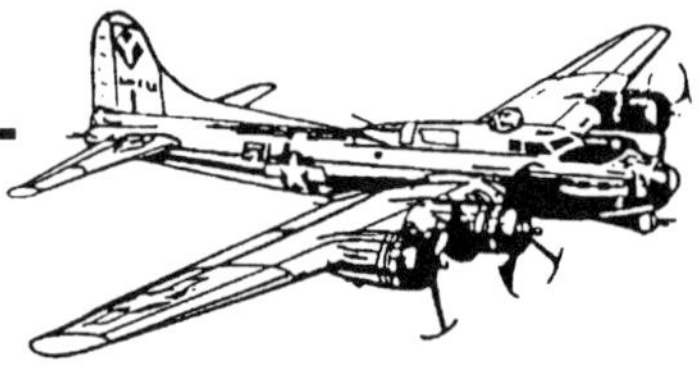

MESSINA, SICILY

MAY 25, 1943

In my logbook for May 25, 1943, a short memo reads: "Bombed oil dump; No. 4 engine hit; lost right aileron; Messerschmitt 210 attack."

There was much more to this mission than those few notes suggest. Not many bomber crews ever experienced a mission like this. Pilots at our base listened in disbelief as they heard how Bankhead, with a crippled bomber, outmaneuvered and out-fought the Nazis' best twin-engine fighter-bomber.

The 25th began with an early assembly of all crews in the briefing test. We were eager to get the scoop on that day's mission. The group itself had flown over twenty bombing missions, with our crew having gone on fifteen of them, and never had enemy planes or anti-aircraft fire been a threat to our group. All planes survived every assault upon them, and our ground crews were accustomed to seeing all our B-17's return to base. Conditions were bound to change.... things were too easy and our lives were uneventful. Wars are not won, or even lost, this way. Someone has to pay the price, something is bound to happen, sooner or later.

Colonel Upthegrove, our commanding officer, speaking in his usual quiet voice, announced that this would be the longest mission to date. It would take us to the oil dumps of Messina, Sicily. Then he casually added, "Gentlemen, this mission is *beyond fighter escort.*" It was to be beyond the fuel range of our P-38 fighters. We stirred in our seats and began to talk to each other in excited stage whispers.

The Colonel pointed out the location of all enemy fighter bases along our route to the target. There were plenty of them. The odds were against us, but the job had to be done. To make matters worse, at the target we could expect enemy fighters to rise up from both Sicily and the mainland of Italy, which was situated only a few miles across the Straits of Messina.

The round trip would be twelve-hundred miles — a long and grueling journey — this meant that we would have to conserve every gallon of fuel; that is, we'd fight for every drop of fuel to return to home base. The flight engineers were instructed to "top off" all tanks after the engines were pre-flighted that morning. This procedure was to insure that no one would run short of fuel. We'd have enough other worries during this seven and one-half hour mission.

We had been pampered long enough. Our previous flights had been half this planned distance, with our stay over hostile territory being less than ten to twenty minutes in duration. Enemy fighters hadn't been too much of a problem, mainly because they were diverted to another target that was struck about fifteen minutes earlier by another American bomber group with considerably more missions to their credit.

The B-17 Bomb Group was the 98th. They came to Africa from bases in England. These were veteran crews in the skills of destroying the German war machine. We respected them. They were serious crews. We were green at bombing, having done practice missions in the past three months.

But now we were going to be tested. It was clear to us that each Fortress would depend on its Gunners and their .50 caliber guns to get through the lengthy gauntlet, and get through twice. "There will be a lot of anti-aircraft fire coming at us during the bomb run," I muttered to my first pilot, H. B. Bankhead. "Batteries in both Sicily and Italy will be zeroing in on our formation."

The weather officer assured us of good flying conditions to the target and on the return trip, as though to infer we would all come back from what seemed like a suicide mission. Then he went through his routine ritual of wishing us "Good luck" — which meant it was time for me to pick up the escape kits for the crew, although the prospects of surviving capture so far from friendly territory seemed remote.

Our escape kits contained cloth maps of Sicily and Italy showing the terrain, rivers, mountains and other data in color. Also encased in the clear heavy plastic were rations of cheese and other non-perishable items to sustain one for several days.

Lt. Bankhead broke the news about the mission to our gunners as we jumped from the Jeep, and, to our surprise, they were enthusiastic. They immediately got to work, checking and rechecking both their weapons and the necessary ammunition. "I want to see more action," said George G. May, our ball turret gunner and assistant radio operator. "I've got confidence in you fellows," I replied. Still, in my own heart, I hated to think about the German Messerschmitts which soon would be boring into our formation from every angle.

Out of twenty-four planes in our group, Lt. Bankhead and I had the unenviable position of being the last plane over the target. We were in the last flight of the last squadron. The flak was always much more accurate, naturally, after the first wave had been measured for altitude. The enemy also had time on the ground to calculate our course. If you were unlucky enough to be crippled by flak — and had to lag behind, you'd be a sitting duck for the enemy fighters who always waited for that very thing to happen. They liked to engage single planes who couldn't keep up with the safety of being in a well-armed formation.

Major Harry Burrell, our squadron commander, was not scheduled for the mission that day. Captain William Clark would lead us. First Lt. Dean Shields led the second element, which included our plane.

Soon we all were airborne and headed for the coast of Africa in the vicinity of Phillipeville. When the armada of twenty-four Fortresses reached the Mediterranean, we were at an altitude of one-thousand feet. (See photo of Bomb Group low over Mediterranean.)

We then dropped to five hundred feet over the water in hopes of escaping detection by enemy radar. As was my custom, I took a last yearning look back toward "home." This time, of course, there was no reassuring umbrella of fighters to escort us. Being in the last plane of the formation, I saw nothing but empty sky. In this theater of war, enemy fighters always concentrated their attacks on the last three planes over the target.

We were in a loose formation, with over two hundred miles of water to navigate before the scheduled climb to the bombing altitude of 23,000 feet when some twenty Messerschmitts began their attack. Apparently, they were from Trapani Air Base in Sicily and they'd been warned of our approach. We had all that distance to go and plenty of trouble already. As we hadn't escaped radar detection, we were ordered to climb to our altitude of 23,000 feet and close up formation.

Photo: from J.F. Bruno Collection

***Above:* The 99th Bomb Group skims low over the Mediterranean on May, 25, 1943 on the way to The MESSINA Mission. The Octopus on our plane, The "PERSUADER" was designed by Navigator, Joe Boyle. This was the last mission for the plane.**

Now we had better firepower, and fortunately for us, all planes operated smoothly as the engines strained at full throttle to get us up to the assigned altitude. Our gunners successfully fought off the first wave of Nazis, with no damage being inflicted upon our planes. After traveling another one hundred miles eastward, more enemy fighters rose to challenge us; but they, too, broke off the attack after a bit of furious action and returned to their bases without causing any damage. The enthusiasm of our gunners was paying off.

Our objective was the supply center for huge amounts of fuel which kept enemy airplanes, tanks, trucks and ships moving constantly against us. Our mission was three and a half nerve-straining hours old when we arrived at the target area. Enemy fighters, warned of our coming long in advance, were up high to meet us. Many diving attacks were made before we could even start the bomb run, but our group would not be driven off. The Colonel stubbornly continued on.

We were seconds away from releasing our bombs when a large puff of black smoke below our right wing turned out to be an accurately- exploding anti-aircraft shell. No. 4 propeller spun wildly out of control. All efforts to feather it were in vain as the burst had struck the oil line at the governor. We managed to keep in formation until the bombs were away, but soon we had to face up to the fact our over-speeding propeller was creating a tremendous drag on the plane. We were in trouble! All efforts to stay beneath the group failed, and the widening gap was immediately noticed by a squadron fighters waiting for just such a situation. The gunners reported eight fighters were attacking.

As the squadron of Messerschmitts singled out our plane for destruction, Joe got on the intercom excitedly asking for help. His impression was that all of them were attacking his area of fire. Bankhead ordered him to get off the intercom and let Jim, the co-pilot, direct the fire.

I had already instructed the gunners to hold their fire until the German fighters were within range. Under no condition, could we afford to waste precious ammunition.

The men settled down and profusely peppered the pursuit squadron with their .50 caliber guns. Sergeant May, our ball turret gunner, exploded one enemy plane and Joe, our navigator, claimed another. Then Jack, the tail gunner, erased number three and our waist gunner, George Diethorn, declared an additional fighter. The battle was fought all the way from the bombing altitude of 23,000 feet down to 10,000 feet. We were steadily losing altitude but the remaining fighters had seen enough of us! They headed back to land, either low on gas or out of ammunition.

Photo: Courtesy Gen. Upthegrove

Oil Dumps of Messina, Sicily on Fire. The Boot of Italy is some five to ten miles to the east of Messina. This was the 25 May, 1943 Mission that Bankhead's crew was crippled down the bomb run. We got our bombs off in unison with the other 23 planes.

Their retreat helped, but, by this time our formation was long out of sight. Another bomber from the 416th squadron had also been damaged. We could hear the pilot report over the radio his flight controls were hit. One of his wing men had dropped back to protect him; now, they would try to determine what could be done to regain control. Not one of our wing men, however, felt it was necessary to drop back to protect us. The flight leader ignored his tail gunner's suggestion to help us. "They're too far gone - they won't make it," he told his gunner.

Having taken the toll of enemy fighters, we prepared to make it back to our base in North Africa. The over-speeding No. 4 propeller was still out of control at 3300 R.P.M., and keeping us from picking up any air speed above 140 M.P.H. The rest of our group made the usual diving turn off the target at the speed of 180 M.P.H. to outdistance the enemy pursuit.

We could faintly see our planes on the western horizon as we resigned to go it alone. Could we make it back over six hundred miles of water in our condition? We were some fifteen minutes away from the target when a deafening vibration threatened to tear off the right wing.

The engine cowlings flew off! We were certain the right wing would shear off next! Bankhead told me to announce instructions over the intercom, "Prepare to bail out!" I no sooner got the words out of my mouth when the propeller lunged forward from the white hot crankcase. I watched it go forward a few feet, then disappear under the wing. In horror, I saw it reappear at the trailing edge of our right wing and slice the aileron in half. The control to the aileron was also severed. Instinctively, both of us reacted by going to full left rudder and left aileron to stay in control.

I did not know what thoughts the other nine men had swirling around in their brains but I remember I prayed to see one more sunset as the sun was going down to the West. It wasn't asking too much; at least it might get us out of the no-win condition facing us.

My entire life flashed before me like a kaleidoscope. I recalled the times I was not kind to my Mother. Of her six children, I had been her favored one and could vividly see her as she would rock me in her lap and sing Italian songs. Would the letter I had written to my sister, Catherine, be mailed for me? Did I write anything the censor would not pass?

Suddenly, my thoughts were interrupted by Bankhead, "Get ready to ditch!"

Our tail gunner, Jack Guerard, did not hear the word, "prepare," he had only heard "Bail Out!" He had already jettisoned his exit door, then decided to crawl back to the waist compartment. No one had bailed out and he learned the "Prepare to bail out!" had been changed to "Prepare for a water landing." He was excitedly happy to not be out over the blue Mediterranean dangling in his parachute while we continued on toward the coast of Africa.

The ditching instructions had been given to us throughout our training. We were instructed to throw all loose items overboard for ditching. Boxes of the remaining ammunition were thrown out. A pair of shoes flew out the window. They would never be needed again - or would they? We all had our water landing "Mae Wests" on. However, I was the only member who had not learned to swim.

The instructor at Sioux City had tried her best to teach me, but to no avail. We moved on to De Ridder, Louisiana before I became able to paddle across the width of the pool. To taunt me, Joe came up to the cockpit while we were still at an altitude of 10,000 feet with his life vest half inflated. "Bruno," he said, "you cannot swim!" Though he seemed to be gloating, I think he felt pity for me. I had to take my chances. We had two life rafts which would deploy from the compartment on each side of the plane. They were located above our pilot area.

Our fervent hope was both would deploy so five men could get into each.

The Mediterranean appeared calm and beautiful from 10,000 feet.

As we descended to 500 feet over the water we saw an angry and rough sea! The waves seemed ready to swallow us and the entire B-17.

It was the co-pilot's duty to call off the airspeed for the landing procedure. I knew as the needle reading on the airspeed indicator came down to 90 miles per hour, the plane would be touching down for the landing. This time it would not be the wheels touching down on a runway. We would be striking the waves, wheels up! I called out the dwindling airspeed of our disabled plane and when 90 miles per hour was called out we were still flying a few feet above the water. With cross controls, the plane should have stalled out and settled into the water at 100 to 105 miles per hour. Our luck was turning for the better. At sea level the engines were functioning at a higher degree of efficiency. They were running much smoother.

The greenish-blue waves surged up seeming to reach out for us. Still, the plane would not make contact with the water. I could not bear to look at the menacing Mediterranean. Minute by minute went by. I quickly glanced at Bankhead. His face showed hope. We were not going to ditch!

He began to inch the throttles ahead. Our airspeed reached 100 miles per hour. It was then I knew we were going to go for the African Coast and make it back to our base.

Our navigator was called from the radio room where all had gathered for the ditching. He was told to give us a heading for home base. We had been flying a westerly direction for the planned ditching. "Give us a course for home," Bankhead said. "We're going to try and make it." We had been flying due west for ditching. Now, we would make a drastic turn to a southerly direction.

Our engineer, also the top turret gunner, was instructed to pump the gas from the Number 4 engine to the tanks of the other three engines. To do this, he had to pump the gas across to the left side of the plane, then transfer it back to the right tank of Number 3 engine. The transfer began, but soon our luck was to change. We saw a twin-engine plane which appeared to come to our rescue. No doubt our radio operator's "MAYDAY" signal was being answered. "It looks like a Bristol Beau-fighter," I said The English used them as fighters and bombers. The plane climbed several thousand feet above us and we soon saw it diving at us from the right side, the co-pilot side. With guns blazing at us, we detected it as the German's best fighter, the feared Messerschmitt 210. It had cannons in the wing and guns which could shoot from the side of the fuselage. "He can do 400 miles an hour," I fretted. I'm not going to enjoy being a clay pigeon for this guy!"

The thought of ditching in hopes the enemy only wanted to claim the plane was quickly abandoned when his first pass came from one o'clock high, with machine guns and wing cannon zeroing in on us. "Thank God! I saved one box of ammo when we jettisoned," said the bombardier. "Just one box! It's in the nose!" The top-turret gunner quickly loaded his guns and the enemy became more cautious in his attack after he almost absorbed a short burst from us. Each time the German fighter went into a dive, Lt. Bankhead would retard the throttles, call for twenty degrees of flaps, and pull up while turning inside the fighter. This would cause our eager enemy to pull up as he began firing, and his shots would go over us. We could see the bullets churning up the water. Had the German chose to come diving to the left of us, we would have been in great danger of stalling out since we could only maneuver the plane and keep flying with left aileron and full left rudder. The enemy was doing us a favor by diving at the co-pilot side of the plane.

After over a half dozen passes aimed at the cockpit, the enemy pilot must have noticed the tail gunner was not firing as he rounded his turn behind our plane. This gave him the chance to strafe us from the rear. He must have known a low pass from behind would cause the upper turret twin fifties to cut out. This was engineered so the guns would not cut through the tail fin of the B-17. Only on a high pass from the rear of the plane would these guns become effective.

His first pass at our plane put a 20 MM cannon shell a few inches over my head. It slammed into the compass correction card encased in a rigid aluminum frame. In that frame, mounted about eighteen inches in front of Bankhead and me was the picture my wife had sent me. She was always smiling at us during all missions. Now, she was the first casualty of war for us. But we were still surviving the enemy.

The pungent odor of smoke from the cannon shell dried our already parched throats. It was difficult to swallow. We were momentarily stunned by the strike inside our cockpit. I was unscathed. I glanced at Bankhead's throttle hand. Blood was spurting from both knuckles. I motioned to take over. He only gripped the throttles tighter, and biting his lip, refused to give up the controls. The handful of shrapnel made him more determined to fight it out to the end.

Continued attacks from the rear of the plane were threatening our eight men huddled in the radio compartment. Only a plywood door separated them from the firepower they were hoping would not strike them. They dove to the floor before the firing began.

Several shells, including cannon shells, did penetrate low enough to strike Fred Manship, who was next to the wood panel. Jack was next to him and felt the shot, though he did escape being injured. Jack and our navigator, Joe, a pre-med student at Boston College, prior to becoming a flying cadet, did what they could for Fred. Ironically, it was Fred's "MAYDAY!" that was answered by the enemy fighter.

The battle for survival was now about twenty minutes old. It was 2:00 P.M. when we began to ditch. The clock inside the cockpit read 2:20 P.M. when it was shattered by the exploding shell.

We were surprised when the enemy stopped strafing from the rear. It was his best target. When he climbed high to target the co-pilot side again, we were once again taken by surprise. He came in low over the cockpit without firing! All of his ammunition had been exhausted. No more cannon fire and no more machine gun fire — a welcome relief.

Our tail gunner, Jack, who had emptied both the .45 guns of the navigator and bombardier now rushed into the cockpit to put an end to the fighter. He snatched my .45 and returned to the radio room. He was ready for the next low level pass over the cockpit. My .45 misfired!

I was able to see the German pilot. He had red hair, a ruddy complexion and a very large grin for us. It seemed he was rocking his wings after passing the cockpit.

Why he never radioed a base on the west coast of Sicily to fly out to finish the job he couldn't do alone was always a mystery to me. We were still some 300 miles from the African Coast.

However, it was at last time for us to again breathe with a sigh of relief. Joe was again called forward to give us a course for home. We had been flying in a westerly direction during the 20 minutes engaging the fighter. A southerly turn to the nearest airport at Tunis was determined. The British had liberated that area two weeks earlier.

While enjoying our good fortune of liberation from enemy guns, our engineer was suddenly reminded that number two tank fuel had been pumping into number three tank for the last twenty minutes. We were about to lose engine number two. At two hundred feet over the water, and flying less than ten miles above stalling airspeed, our plane and crew would have met a watery grave. The transfer valve was quickly shut off and fuel was returned to our number two engine. Our fuel gauges told us they would be showing the "Red - Danger" spot on the dial before long. Ditching was not an option! We had to get Freddie to a hospital. Normally, a mixture of fuel to the engines would be leaned as we flew at higher altitude. We took the chance and leaned the mixture flying above the water.

The coast of Africa was very welcome sight. The gauges told us we had to land. The airport was sighted. It was a short fighter strip. There was no time or reason to circle as one would do at a strange field. A flare was fired to announce we had wounded on board. A slight turn to the right put us in line for the landing. Bankhead had a tricky job of releasing just enough left aileron pressure and left rudder pressure to level off so both wheels would touch down smoothly.

The landing was beautiful; however, the railroad embankment at the end of the runway was coming up fast!

We went for the foot brakes - they moved to the floor! The hydraulic lines had been damaged by the enemy. Bankhead instantly reached behind us and jerked down the Emergency brake handles.

The plane was brought to a stop less than fifteen feet from the embankment! Who, in their right mind, would plan a runway with a railroad embankment at one end?!

By the time we taxied back to the hangar area, a British ambulance was waiting.

Our first priority was to get Freddie into the ambulance for the trip to the hospital. Despite having lost an enormous amount of blood, he was still conscious. I stood outside the waist compartment window as he was handed out. My outstretched hand could barely cover the gaping wound in his spine. The compress was soaked and the oozing blood covered my hand.

He thanked us as he was placed on the stretcher and said he was glad we got back to the coast. He was rushed to the hospital in Tunis at 5:30 P.M.

There was little reason for the hospital or emergency staff to be on duty as the Germans were gone. It was time for them to enjoy some time off. About four hours passed before the orderlies could turn Fred over to a doctor.

Bankhead's first thought after the fighter left was to head for Cape Bone as the hospital there had good medical facilities and was in Allied hands for a long period of time. With our fuel dangerously low, we knew the hospital, 125 miles west of Tunis was out of range of the fuel remaining.

Bankhead rode along in the ambulance to have his right hand taken care of. The shrapnel was not removed. He returned with a bandaged hand. The rest of the crew awaited him and together we secured quarters for the night. The officers were given a third floor room accommodating four. The enlisted men were given a first floor room.

We were testing the mattresses when we heard a loud bang. Instinctively, all four of us dived under the beds;. It was the sound we heard when the cannon shells were pounding us. The bang, we learned, was the backfiring of a motorcycle on the street below!

Bankhead went to the hospital around midnight to check up on Fred's condition. He returned with the disheartening words that Fred did not survive. Here was a cheerful young man, who never lost consciousness, in an insufferable ordeal at a hospital without life-saving equipment. Bankhead said later, "A well man could have died in that hospital!"

It was a disturbing night of rest for all the crew. The next morning we inquired about transportation back to home base. The U.S. Army provided a truck and driver. Our personal items and parachutes were loaded and we travelled the 150 miles. There was no facility to notify home base that we had made it back from Messina where we were last seen.

You can imagine the surprised faces as the truck with our nine survivors drove to our tent. Word circulated fast that Bankhead was back. Our squadron commander, Harry Burrell, was the happiest. He was concerned about writing to my wife, Irene, and having to tell her I did not survive the Messina mission. Irene was his favorite, and the other wives knew it when we were back in the States. Harry would play the piano for the dances with Irene sitting on one side of him and I on the other. Irene was always his first choice for a dance when he would put a dime in the juke box. The other wives waited their turn.

Our flight leader was not too happy to see us. He had removed both my mattress and Bankhead's from our cots and given them to other officers. Before long, he sheepishly returned them to us.

A few days later we heard Bankhead was recommended for the Silver Star. The rest of us were recommended for the Distinguished Flying Cross. It came as a surprise. The only medals handed out to date were for the Purple Heart.

The awards were later changed. Bankhead received the Distinguished Flying Cross. The remaining members of the crew would not receive the DFC. None of us were upset, however, because we felt Bankhead deserved the Silver Star for his heroic performance in handling the crippled plane and out-performing the German fighter pilot.

Telegrams were sent to our families the night before, stating we were "Missing in Action," since 25, May.

The week of our landing in Tunis, a crew of mechanics was sent to examine our plane. With no spare plane to go on missions, we took a Jeep to Tunis. The mechanics found an unexploded 20 MM cannon shell in number three tank. It was given to Bankhead as a souvenir. The compass correction card with the shattered photo of my wife was given to me.

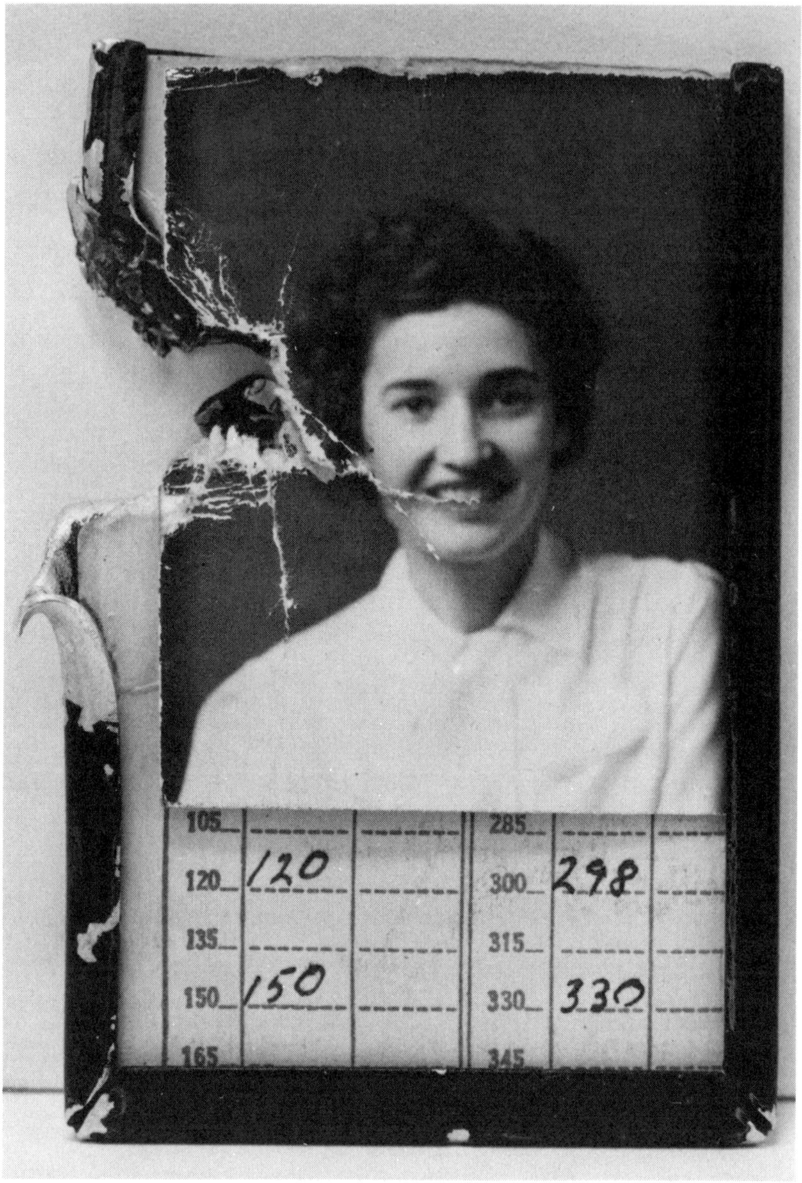

Photo: J.F. Bruno Collection

Author's Wife, Irene. Photo was displayed in compass correction card located between pilot and co-pilot station. 20 mm cannon shell entered cockpit over Author's head and exploded on impact with compass correction card. Pilot Bankhead received shrapnel in throttle hand and kept flying the plane.

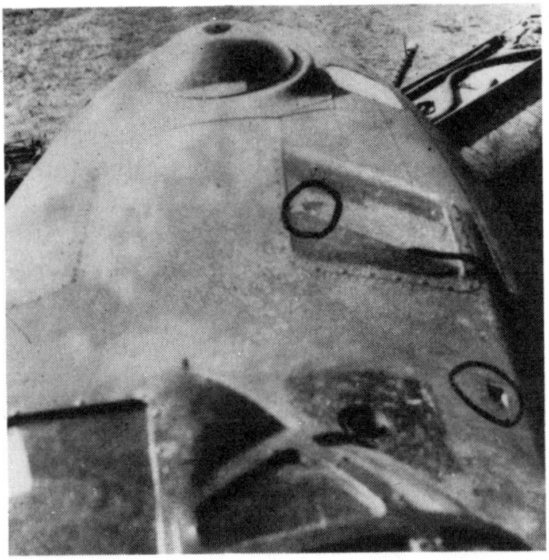

Cannon shell that entered over authors head that exploded on impact with aluminum compass correction card holding picture of Author's wife

CREW OF THE PERSUADER

Front row left to right: T/Sgt. James J. Florek, Engineer Chicago, IL; Lt. David L. Fronefield, Bombardier Patterson, NJ; Lt. H.B. Bankhead, Pilot Wellesville, UT; Lt. James F. Bruno, Co-Pilot Waukesha, WI; Lt. Joseph A. Boyle, Navigator Boston, MA.

Standing, left to right: S/Sgt. Frank J. Kovac, Asst. Engineer Monica, PA; Sgt. George H. Diethorn, Gunner Highland Park, MI; S/Sgt. George G. May, Asst. Radio Operator Utica, NY; T/Sgt. Melvin E. Hall, Radio Operator Van Buren, IN; S/Sgt. Jack D. Guerard, Tail Gunner Beaufort, SC.

Photo: James F. Bruno Collection

PERSUADER AT TUNIS, NORTH AFRICA

Mechanics of the 347th Squadron survey battle damage of May 25, 1943. Holes near Navigators compartment made by anti-aircraft burst over Messina, Sicily. Light spots on Number 2 engine propeller are from German Fighter guns during 20 minute fight when enemy shifted attack to rear of bomber. Shrapnel almost pierced thick aluminum propeller.

Photo: J.F. Bruno Collection

PERSUADER BATTLE DAMAGE AT TUNIS

A Tunisian family looks on in disbelief after Persuader landed at the airfield less than ten days after the Germans had been driven out of North Africa.

Note the disabled Right Aileron damaged near Messina, Sicily that was cut in half and put out of control by the falling propeller. The crew returned over 350 miles over water and fought the Germans best Twin-engine fighter on their return trip.

RESTRICTED

HEADQUARTERS NORTHEAST AFRICAN AIR FORCES A. P. O. 650

GENERAL ORDERS) 8 Aug 1943

NUMBER 158)

EXTRACT

Award of The Distinguished Flying Cross I
Award of Oak Leaf Cluster for Distinguished Flying Cross . . II

Section I - AWARDS OF DISTINGUISHED FLYING CROSS

Under the provisions of AR 600-45, as amended, and persuant to authority contained in Cir. No. 128, NATOUSA, 8 July,1943, the Distinguished Flying Cross is awarded to the following named personnel, Air Corps,United States Army, residence and citizen as indicated, in the name of the Commanding General NATOUSA:

* * * * * * * * * *

HEBER B. BANKHEAD, 0434064, 1st Lt,Wellesville,Utah. For extraordinary achievement while participating in aerial flight in the North African theatre of Operations as pilot of a B-17 type aircraft. Over Messina on 25 May, 1943, Lt. Bankhead's plane was severely damaged and forced out of formation by anti-aircraft fire. He successfully engaged six enemy fighters, three of which were destroyed by members of his crew. Further damage to his B-17 necessitated the disposal of all guns and amunition in order to maintain flight altitude. While in this defenseless condition he was attacked by an enemy plane, and disregarding a painful wound in one hand, he so skifully and inteligently employed evasive tactics that the enemy aircraft withdrew, and the bomber and all members were subsequently landed in friendly territory. His expert judgement and flying ability under extreme conditions reflect great credit upon himself and the Armed Forces of the United States.

* * * * * * * *

By command of Lieutenant General SPAATZ:

E.P.CURTIS,
Brigadier General
Chief of Staff

OFFICIAL: /s/ WILLIAM W. DICK
Colonel, A.G.D.
Air Adjutant General.

RESTRICTED

99th Bomb Group Awards Presentation
Bankhead in the line to receive the Distinguished Flying Cross and Purple Heart. June 13,1943.

Author's wife Irene one year later at Ellington Field, Texas

THE GERMAN AIR FORCE - A BAG OF TRICKS

We made many unescorted missions to Italy from our base far from the African Coast. On one mission, Bankhead and I observed a German fighter engaged in a dogfight with a P-38. I told Bankhead, "That P-38 does not belong here over Italy. It is out of range to return to Africa." When we returned to our base, word had gotten to us that the P-38 was flown by a German pilot. The dogfight was staged. The P-38 shot into the cockpit of one of the B-17's (not ours) and killed both pilots.

Also from the Eighth Air Force, we learned the Germans had a B-17. They would fly it at the altitude of our bombers and being out of range of our .50 caliber guns, would call off speed and altitude to the anti-aircraft batteries on the ground.

OUR CREW GOES TO REST CAMP

After our harrowing Messina Mission and being without our B-17, "The Persuader," the decision was made to send the crew to rest camp. It was unheard of to this date. If we had any "battle fatigue," we were not aware of it. However, none of the crew objected to the resort where we were to spend the next ten days.

A C-47 transport plane picked us up at the bomber base on July 6th and flew us to Casablanca where we stayed overnight. We were in no mood to explore the Kasbah that evening. Maybe the battle fatigue was setting in. Our navigator, Joe, never passed up a chance to visit a night club or bar to sample the beer and visit with the patrons. The next morning we were flown to the resort city of Agadir, about 200 miles south of Casablanca. The Red Cross ran the resort.

Accommodations were first-class and the hotel rivaled most of the hotels in the States. It was built on a hillside overlooking the Atlantic Ocean. A winding road brought us up to the fifth level where the registration desk, bar and dining room were located.

A French Officers Club a block away from the hotel had a movie theater and the usual Officers Bar where we rubbed shoulders with men of the French Foreign Legion. They were very gentle soldiers - so it seemed to us. The Red Cross ladies took us on tours by bus to various towns which everyone enjoyed. The palaces and buildings rivaled the architecture and splendor of the United States. Of course, we had no Kings or Arab Sheiks in the United States either. Frankly, we were all anxiously looking forward to returning to our group and receiving our new B-17.

Being a curious fellow, it wasn't long before I decided to check the winding, narrow streets of the city.

A "Brower Shoes" sign, a familiar name to me in the States caught my eye. Upon entering the shop, an engagingly attractive young Arab lady asked, "May I show you some shoes?" My interest in shoes disappeared as I tried to tell her we had a "Brower's" in my home town. Becoming acquainted with her would be far more interesting than any pair of shoes I had in my lifetime to date! As we talked, I asked her if she would like to accompany me to dinner at the Club? She shook her head from side-to-side and replied, "Your Officers Club is 'off limits' to the Arab people here."

Several days later, a worker at the hotel remarked to me the winsome French barmaid looked very sad. I asked the young lady, "Why so sad?" She answered, "My boyfriend, the Sergeant, has been transferred." I assumed, before that morning, this unusually pretty woman was the wife of the head bartender. After a brief conversation, I offered my consolation, wished her well and left.

A few days later three other officers and I returned to the Club to while away the evening and browse around with our French Foreign Legion friends. In our conversations, I mentioned the alluring barmaid would have made a "great date" for one of our men.

Leaving to return to our hotel, I received a severe tongue lashing from Joe about not telling him about what could have been "a great French date" for someone. We flew out the next morning with Joe's scathing words still ringing in my ears!

We were tiring of the Red Cross tours and the French Officers Club, longing to return to our new B-17. The country club life was becoming uninteresting to us. There was a job left to do and 34 unfinished missions looming ahead for me. The other fellows were not too far behind me. I was put on extra missions as bombardier when the crew I belonged to were not scheduled. At the discretion of the scheduling department, I flew as co-pilot for other first pilots.

There were some crews who left for the States as early as July, 1943. Departing after their 50 missions gave them six months overseas from the time we left the States in February. Don't think we didn't envy them!

On the day we returned, our new plane had not yet arrived. I was put on as bombardier. The target? Messina again! The crew? The same ones who left us to return alone with our crippled plane as a target for a squadron of German fighters!

My loved ones were notified 21 days later that I returned to duty the same day I was reported Missing in action.

Authors Note: About ten years after the end of the war, an article appeared in the Milwaukee Journal that the City of Agadir had been rocked by an earthquake. Being on a rocky hillside along the Atlantic Ocean, the report went on to say the city was demolished!

CHAPTER 7

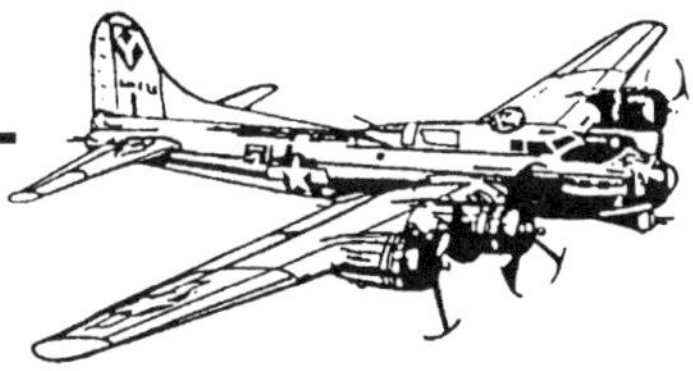

GERBINI, SICILY

GERBINI AIRDROME MISSION
JULY 5, 1943

The Allies were preparing for the invasion of Italy when they decided on a 4th of July celebration by destroying one of Sicily's largest fighter bases. This mission was also beyond the range of our American fighters. The British Spitfires based on the Island of Malta set to meet us at a predetermined area over the Mediterranean and south of Sicily. Some sixty Spitfires were assigned as escort. Major Warren Whitmore of the 348th Squadron was to lead our group. The 98th Bomb Group and the 301st were also on this mission.

Bankhead and I were in the last element of twenty-four planes of our group. With a total of 75 planes for this mission, we felt secure about returning from the important raid. With the gallant record of the British Spitfires, we were doubly secure. Captain Harry Burrell was leading the 347th Squadron.

Little did we know (we later found out) orders had come down from Nazi General Hermann Goering directing their fighters to shoot down the last three B-17's of the formation. Somehow, the lead navigator in Major Whitmore's lead plane miscalculated and the rendezvous point and the Spitfires were not sighted. Major Whitmore wisely decided to return to the base in Africa and, in so doing, the mission was aborted. That navigational error probably saved our lives, as we learned the next day.

On July 5th, the mission was rescheduled. This time, Colonel Upthegrove decided to lead the mission. Captain Bob Elliott was to lead the 348th Squadron. Bankhead and I were also reshuffled to be up front and to the right of the Colonel's squadron. I believe he guessed our gunners would protect his plane by pouring plenty of their lead into the enemy fighters. He, too, was unaware of the orders to shoot down the last three B-17's.

The rendezvous was accomplished at the agreed point and altitude over the Mediterranean and all planes proceeded on a northerly course into the central part of Sicily. The toughest battle with the enemy was about to begin.

Long before the target was in sight, swarms of Messerschmitts were ready to defend their base. Aerial bombs were dropped which exploded in front of us. Messerschmitts and Italian fighters tried to split up the squadron and cripple as many planes as they could.

We heard continuous excited bits of chatter over the intercom. Our gunners complained the Spitfires were coming through the formation and shooting at us. Some one hundred Messerschmitts and sixty Spitfires were coming at us. Who could keep track in that inferno of blazing machine guns? In the heat of the attack, Colonel Upthegrove calmly lead us down the bomb run and bombs were accurately dropped on our section of the field and hangers.

The diving turn off the target was always a welcome relief after bombs away. Soon, we heard our planes at the rear squadron were under heavy fighter attack. Men were instructed to bail out when the plane could no longer be maneuvered. Of the twenty-four planes Colonel Upthegrove brought over the target, he was now returning to the base in Africa with twenty-one. We were all hoping the thirty crew members who were not so lucky had bailed out and were not injured.

Back at our base, the debriefing with gunners and pilots was conducted. A total of 36 enemy planes was claimed to have been shot down. The gunners who were shot down claimed 11 enemy planes, as shown by the press release. That would give the Spitfires 4 enemy planes. These are estimated figures.

Several days later, we heard the German pilots had visited our wounded airmen in the hospital. The German pilots admitted they lost 51 planes. To my knowledge, we did not learn how many Spitfires were lost nor the number of enemy planes they destroyed. From my front row seat, those Spitfires put up one heroic fight to protect us that day

Authors note. (I read several years after the war that the island of Malta was one of the most heavily bombed islands by the Nazis. It sustained over two thousand air strikes as it lay across the route of supplies being shipped to North Africa.)

The account of the fate of the last three B-17's and their crews is vividly written here by Intelligence Officer Captain Hutchison of our group. General Upthegrove sent me this in our correspondence in 1970.

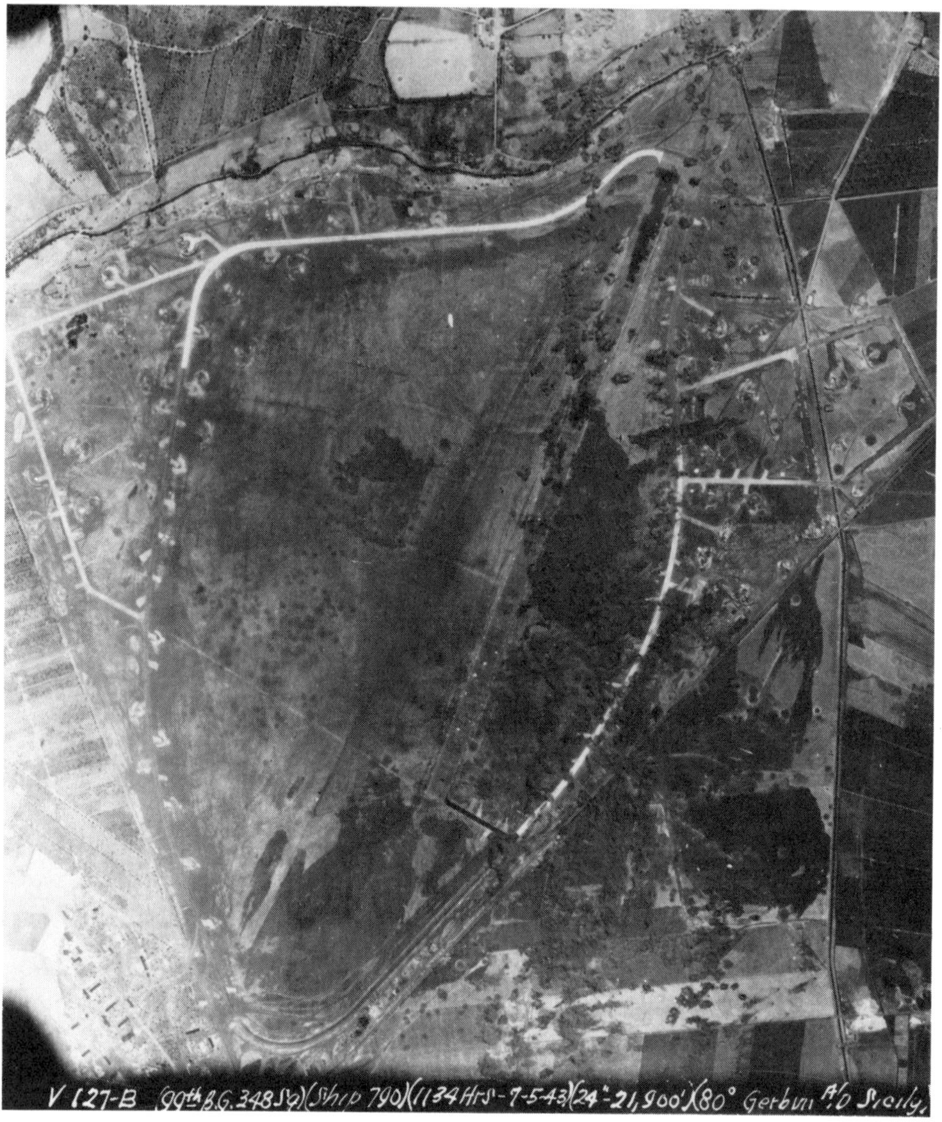

Gerbini Airdrome, photo 7-5-43 99th Bomb Group 348th Squadron. Photo from 21,900 Ft.

The 348th Squadron lost their last three B-17's to German fighters that day.

HEADQUARTERS
NINETY-NINTH BOMBARDMENT GROUP (H) ARMY AIR FORCES

Office of the Intelligence Officer

19 July, 1943

PRESS RELEASE: By Captain G. E. Hutchison

Two heavy bombardment crew members were sprawled across their cots today in a North African hospital pinching themselves to see if it was all true and that they were really alive and back in a building over which flew the Stars and Stripes. They were receiving plaudits of privates and colonels from their group alike as if they had arisen from the dead to bring back word of a fortnight's nightmarish episode in which they and members of three entire crews had been practically given up for dead after having been shot down over Sicily at the outbreak of the Allied invasion of the island at the toe of Italy's boot.

Today the boot was on the other foot for Staff Sergeant, Allen B. Huckabee, at 42 believed to be the oldest gunner in the North African theater (770 North Seventh St., Temple, Texas) and flak-riddled Technical Sergeant, David Flemming, 1405 South Milwaukee St , Jackson, Michigan, radio operator.

With four men already killed in their B-17 after an attack by more than 100 enemy pursuit ships during a raid over the main airdrome at Gerbini, Sicily, at noon on July 5, and their guns shot out by flak and 20 mm shells, Huckabee, Fleming and five others bailed out to be captured only a few minutes later by Italian troops.

But let them tell the story:

"We were about five minutes after the target when a swarm of Italian and German planes jumped us. They were coming at us from all directions in groups of two, three and four. We were riding in the lead plane of the second element. At about this time the flak began popping around us like a belated Fourth of July celebration and we knew we were in for a battle. Finally our number four engine caught fire and we couldn't feather the props which slowed us down to about 110 miles an hour. The entire formation slowed down to cover us but soon our second engine was shot out and we were slowed to a stalling speed. The plane on the right wing pulled in close to us but it seemed like his motors were running away.

"Just at this time our tail gunner came crawling through the fuselage. He was bleeding and we could see that he was shot in the stomach. We couldn't do a thing for him because we were all so busy.. The boy stood up and helped our left waist gunner feed the shells and all of a sudden he toppled over dead."

"The ball turret gunner came crawling out his left leg below the knee gone and a deep wound in his left chest. It was only a matter of seconds and he was gone."

Huckabee told how he looked through to the front of the ship and saw the co-pilot leaning against the pilot. He said he left his guns long enough to go up and pull him away only to find him dead too, a deep ugly hole in his right chest.

Huckabee said he kept firing at the seemingly endless rush of fighter planes when he looked around and saw his fellow waist gunner lying dead with a hole in his head and a deep gash on one of his shoulders.

"The noise was terrific," they said.

"The bullets and shells sounded like rice in a tin can. We were losing altitude and finally our pilot, who incidentally did the greatest job we ever saw told us to jump." About this time a 20 mm shell came through the fuselage and lodged in the lower part of Huckabee's back.

which knocked us out. We came to and hurriedly buckling on our parachute equipment we made for the door only to find it wedged shut. We managed to make for the windows and climbed out. We were down to about 5,000 feet when we took to the silk.

"As we were going down all the pursuit except three seemed to disappear. These three kept circling around us all the time we were going down. We did see more parachutes in the air and we are sure they were from the ship on our right wing which was having engine trouble back early in the battle. We later saw the plane crash land in flames on a beach."

"When we hit, some farmers ran out and came to a halt at a distance until we motioned them to come on over. Reluctantly they came over and finally they picked us up and carried us over to their farm yard The five others who had bailed out of our plane rejoined us. The Sicilians gave us water and blankets but after about 10 minutes soldiers in civilian clothing leaped over the fence and with guns drawn made us prisoners. They searched us and pretty soon an Italian Red Cross ambulance came along and took us to a Catholic hospital about five miles away and 15 miles from Ragusa. There they gave us first aid and dressed our wounds. It was now about two o'clock in the afternoon."

"The first thing they did was to put the two of us in a ward. We were the only ones injured. The five others, who didn't get a scratch, were taken to another part of the building. That was the last we saw of them but we later learned from a pilot they had been flown to a prisoner of war camp near Venice, Italy."

"Next they tried to interrogate us. We were first asked our names, rank and serial numbers. We replied we were not paratroopers and they asked us if we had been in on any of the Palermo or Messina raids. They were plenty mad about these two raids, claiming 200,000 had been killed in Palermo alone from raids by heavy bombardment groups."

"First a Colonel interrogated us. We found out later that he was the first to surrender when Ragusa was captured by the Americans. He asked us where our group was located and to the question "how many planes are the Americans turning out every day" we answered, "30,000". That made him plenty mad and he called us liars. Finally he stormed; "Don't you ignorant Americans know better than to try to conquer Italy and Germany."

"We just laughed and snickered and he got real mad and brushed out of the room in a huff. Next a civilian interrogated us and about every other question was; "Did you bomb Palermo?"

"They took everything away from us, even our dog tags. We were like two monkeys in a cage. Everyone tried to take a look at us. They even climbed up on the outside wall to peer through the foot-square iron-barred window. That afternoon the Colonel brought a lot of his friends down to show us off, even to his little daughter."

"They kept pounding us with questions. "How many men have you in Africa? How many planes have you there? Where is your base? How many raids have you been on?" These were only a few."

"We had an orderly 24 hours a day who was instructed to get us anything we wanted, within reason. Two guards were at our bedside. We stayed there all that night and the next day they moved us to the International Red Cross Hospital at Ragusa. Two miles from the hospital, American bombers came over and we "sweated it out" under a cliff for an hour until the raiders were gone."

"There was a lot of red tape getting us in the hospital but once we got in they treated us royally. They took us to the operating room and dressed our wounds. Then they started asking us more questions but we feigned great pain so they laid off. We had a guard placed around us but we learned later the guard wasn't placed there to keep us from escaping. We were being guarded from fanatics who carried the grudge of the Palermo raid."

"Then came the day when the Americans took Ragusa. The city had a population of 50,000. It was all done by 17 G.I.'s and three jeeps and you can put that down as official. The night before the invasion they told us the Americans were coming. You should have seen the two guards clear out. Then all the Italian wounded and sick came to us and asked us to have the Americans spare them. They had been told they would be slaughtered when and if the Americans came."

"The first we knew the Americans were there was shortly before daybreak when a sergeant came in swaggering with a tommy-gun. He "took" the hospital single handedly."

"It was not long that the Italians were really glad the Yankees had come. But the next morning about 9:30 they started shelling the city and we had to run for cover. We all went down into the basement."

"Finally we worked up enough nerve to go out and steal a jeep. We drove two blocks to the post office where the American headquarters were located. Mind you, all this time we had on pajamas and had them on to this very day."

"We got some "C" rations and laid down in a doorway. Finally some Canadians came in and we went back to the hospital. There we got an ambulance and drove to Comiso another headquarters the United States had established. A major took us to a hotel and then a colonel came in and brought along a public relations officer and a newspaper man."

"We stayed there that night and the next day we started out with a corporal as our driver for the clearing station hospital. On the way we saw four German dive-bombers come in for a landing on a field that had been taken over by the allies. The Germans didn't know this and when they were about to land the boys on the field opened up on them. Well, there wasn't much left of those four planes so we drove on."

"Reaching the clearing hospital, they dressed our wounds again. Then they decided to move us to an evacuation hospital on the beach 15 miles away. It took us four hours to make those 15 miles in a Red Cross ambulance. The driver got lost and once when we drove along a lane we were set upon by snipers. The shots seemed to come from all directions. They couldn't have mistaken the ambulance because there was a full moon and the Red Cross Stood out prominently.

"We made the beach and then all of a sudden there was an air raid. Luck surely was with us for none of the sniper's bullets or frags from the bombs touched us. We finally got to the hospital and they gave us a tetanus shot."

"The next day they loaded nine of us wounded soldiers on a transport along with 400 prisoners and "we took off for Tunis but we had to go by way of the Balkans to make it because of the mined waters. Thirty hours later we reached Tunis. An ambulance took us to a hospital in Tunis and after two days they loaded us on a hospital train and brought us here."

"The Red Cross at Ragusa sent word to our families we were wounded prisoners of war and the Red Cross at Tunis notified them we were safe. It was while we were at the evacuation hospital on the beach that they awarded us each the Purple Heart. It was all done without ceremony."

"The Italians told us we shot down 51 of their planes in that fight. We were given credit for 38 and we claimed 50 we heard later. We know our crew shot down 11."

That is the saga of the first two Americans to be returned to Africa after having been captured by the Italians in the Sicilian invasion.

But that saga does not near tell the anxiety and hopes which were wafted up and down with the North African winds, hopes which in time became only wishful for the 400 buddies of the three crews back at their base.

A few held out hope they would be heard from again. As many declared they would never come back, knowing too well the ferocity of the attack of flak and machine guns that day over Gerbini. Yes, it was like voices from the dead to hear those two gallant crewmen relate their harrowing experiences from their bedside, voices which have buoyed the hopes of the 400 the same day they will hear from the other 30 who are listed as "missing in action".

THE INVASION OF SICILY - JULY 9, 1943
(The Secret Night Mission)

Captain Bankhead and I, as co-pilot, were slated to be on the night mission with our crew and special equipment on board to jam the German radar. We needed to cover the U.S. Army paratroopers who were supported by the U.S. Naval Fleet. Flying up and down the Sicilian coastline at night was not a "milk-run" by any means. The crew accepted the challenge.

When morning came, Captain Burrell decided he and another crew would fly the night mission instead. We had no objection.

From what Colonel Upthegrove wrote of that perilous mission, we were fortunate to have been outranked and left at the base.

(Our Colonel wrote this in our newsletter.) "I don't remember the four planes used, whether they were all the 99th, or part of the air force. I believe the pilots chosen used their own crews or parts of same. I had so many worries connected with the safety of our planes in the path of dozens of C-47's, British glider tows and naval ships below that each crew had to be responsible for their plane and crews."

Those elements were: the Airborne element of paratroopers using C-47 planes, the Glider elements of the

British, and the U.S. Naval forces. This was to be the initial landing of ground forces in Sicily. Radar jamming and first night B-17's equipped with black boxes were used with technicians furnished by Headquarters North American African Air Forces.

All turns were to be gentle and made to the left to keep our flight as simple as possible. We had to trust the Troop Carrier and Glider people to keep the 500′ and 1500′ altitudes assigned. (Burrell saw a Glider tow pass close to him but that was all.)

I don't remember the number of C-47's lost and men killed by our Navy nor the number of Gliders and men lost, but they were considerable.

I was so tired from loss of sleep and the running around that the mission was about the worst we flew in the entire time. It was much more nerve wracking than Gerbini or Palermo.

(Author 's Comments)

"While that night mission and landing by our paratroopers was quite successful, I read in our veterans publications that two nights after the air drop, General Patton ordered the remainder of the 82nd Airborne to Sicily. This proved to be one of the most tragic mistakes of the war."

"As the transport planes approached the beach, they passed over an American flotilla still at battle stations following a German bomber attack. The 144 troop transports carrying over 2,000 men were fired upon by Allied anti-aircraft batteries who mistook them for German bombers. Twenty-three (23) C-47's were shot down by friendly fire causing the death of some 300 paratroopers." (Radio silence had its advantages; however, there were also disadvantages.)

GERBINI AIRDROME RAID, JULY 5, 1943

This is the July 5th Group Formation

346-Stephigh

Upthegrove
313

Hugo-a 344 | **Bliss-b** 512

Aspergren-d
526

Mehew-h 477 | **Ebbers-i** 3129

Lippman-c
513

347-Swanlake

Burrell-o
384

Shields-k 473 | **Hager-p** 480

Covert-n
769

Moseley-q 786 | **Bankhead-b** 164

Stuart-m
746

416-Windscreen

Orance-t
507

Mitchell-v 509 | **Was-s** 482

Thistlewood-w
765

Norris-u 413 | **Buck-c** 883

Windrum-a
472

348-Shortcut

Elliott-f
790

Davis WC-s 842 | **Casto-l** 857

Davis-AE-i
483

***Graham-d** 492 | ***Samuelson-i** 388

***Devane-h**
486

*(Shot Down)

CHAPTER 8

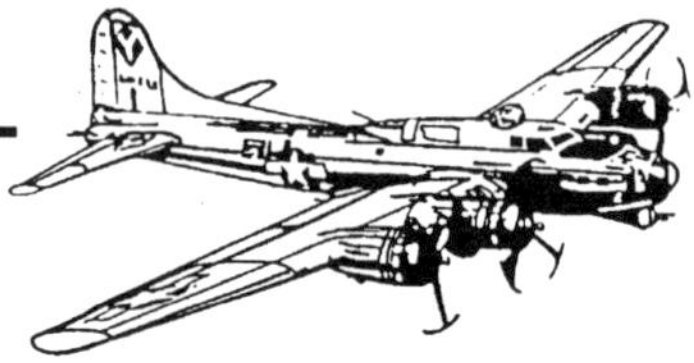

ROME, FOGGIA, INSERNIA AND FROSINONE

THE BOMBING OF ROME
JULY 19, 1943

The announcement we would bomb Rome created quite a stir in the group, and for some reason or another we all wanted to be included in this dramatic effort. Bankhead and I were picked to be both "camera ship" and "radio ship" for the mission. We would lead the second element of the squadron, with the squadron to be the second flight of six planes.

We studied the information on our target carefully. It was the famous railroad yards of Rome, filled to capacity with war supplies, as could be expected. This was a golden opportunity to deal the enemy a severe blow, if we could get through. Maps were distributed to the navigators, and the course was accurately laid out on the briefing room wall.

These maps gave the exact location of the Vatican in relation to the railroad yards. The best heading for the bomb run took us directly toward the Vatican. If we were to avoid the disaster of having bombs fall on the Holy City, we would have to release our bombs at precisely the right second. If any bombardiers were to miss the aiming point, our 500-pounders would harm the Vatican and its people, and the moral and political repercussions would be on our shoulders. It was a sobering responsibility to all of us.

The flight took us over surprisingly light anti-aircraft fire, and only a few enemy fighters stormed up to challenge us. The weather was clear and the mission went off as briefed. Our photographs showed that we blew up many freight cars full of supplies, along with some-hard-to-replace locomotives. Only two bombs went over the boundaries of the yards, and then by a mere fifty to a hundred feet. Not a single bomb fell on the Vatican. We had done a fine job. This was one of many missions where the skilled teamwork of the navigator, the pilot, and the bombardier combines to deliver the bombs directly and effectively onto the target.

This mission was one where the bomber groups had press coverage to make sure no bombs went astray. Tech Sergeant Melvin E. Hall's radio message alerted the outside world bombs were being dropped on the City of Rome. We also had the photographer on board our B-17.

Although the 500 plane raid on the railroad yards was accurate pinpoint bombing, the Italian Government Propaganda reported that we had destroyed the Vatican.

Here, by permission of the OMAHA WORLD-HERALD, is the accurate account of the raid and mission:

OMAHA WORLD-HERALD

Five Planes Lost in 500 - Plane Whip Lash Assault on Rome compiled from Cable Dispatches

While axis propagandists beat the drums of indignation,

allied headquarters in North Africa described Monday's shattering aerial assault on Rome as an "outstandingly successful" operation and disclosed officially tuesday that more than five hundred bombers carried out the raid with a loss of only five planes.

Aerial reconnaissance showed heavy damage to all targets and a Ninth United States Air Force communique from Cairo said the Littoria railroad yards "were completely destroyed."

The Tabonelli steel plant and a large chemical works were battered by the waves of American raiders which swept over Rome for two and a half hours, challenged by what was described officially as only "slight opposition" from enemy fighter planes.

Two enemy interceptors were blasted out of the air by Lightning fighters which escorted the heavy and medium bombers.

Thanks to perfect weather and explicit instructions given to crews, the objectives were easily spotted, and the bomb loads were dropped with pinpoint accuracy.

Lt. Marion D. Jones of Memphis, Tenn., flying his fiftieth mission, said his formation found no difficulty in keeping away from the forbidden points.

"We thought we'd have to be very careful to hit only military objectives," he said, "but there was nothing to it. We saw Vatican City about five miles across the river from the railroads and the industrial regions."

Many are Catholics

Many of the airmen who participated were members of the Catholic faith. Some acknowledged they were worried about the Vatican but others saw the city as a perfectly legitimate target.

Maj. Warren Whitmore of Jacksonville, Fl., said he was worried more about possible anti-aircraft defense than the problem of spotting his target.

"We had been very carefully briefed and I knew I could depend on the navigator to pinpoint our target and the bombardier to smack it on the nose," he said.

"Besides, my second in command Bob Elliot, is a devout Catholic, and he felt good about going, so when I saw that I just stopped worrying."

The successive waves of bombers swept inland over the capital following the snake-like Tiber River.

They reported there was evidence that the Italians had taken steps to protect some of the landmarks against a possible raid. The columns of the Trajan arch of Titus and the cascades, which are ornamented by Bernini sculptures, appeared to be encased in heavy concrete.

No Opposition

On one plane over Rome the radio operator heard the British announcement of the bombing. He tuned in the German stations and heard an announcement in English that the Vatican had been destroyed.

What surprised the American flyers most was the absence of Italian aerial opposition.

Anti-aircraft fire was moderate to heavy, pilots said, but inaccurate.

The Italians made heated charges that "buildings sacred to faith and science" had been heavily hit and the Germans threatened retaliation

The Italian communique, placing the toll of victims at 166 killed and 1,659 injured, declared that 11 historic buildings had been heavily hit.

Threaten Retaliation

Unconfirmed reports said that General Hazon, the supreme commander of Italian military police, had been killed with his Chief Aide, Colonel Barenco.

Among the places partly destroyed, the communique said, were the San Lorenzo Basilica, Verano Cemetery, University City and hospitals of the Polyclinic Institute.

Dr. Paul Schmidt, German foreign office spokesman, was quoted by the Berlin radio Tuesday as saying:

"The day will come for which everyone in Germany and Italy is waiting - the day which we are determined will come; The day of revengeful retaliation when the cup of hatred will finally overflow."

Dr Schmidt explained that his declarations "should not be regarded as an appeal to world opinion but as an expression of iron determination to retaliate."

One typical outburst came from a German radio commentator, Otto Krieg, who said in a broadcast recorded by the Associated Press; "Throughout the world today there is but one theme on the cry of indignation. Rome has been bombed by terror raiders, crooks and gangsters."

THE ROME SAN LORENZO RAIL ROAD YARDS

The dotted area contains the heaviest damage. Reconnaissance planes recorded the damage three hours after the raids. The Vatican City and St. Paul's Cathedral (below the letters "ZO") are in the upper left, untouched by the bombs.

Photo: Courtesy of General Upthegrove

THE BOMBING OF ROME - 19 JULY, 1943

LITTORIO MARSHALLING YARDS - Photo from 31,000 ft.

Our plane took photos and was the Radio Voice that announced the bombing to the outside world (T/Sgt. Melvin Hall announced the Bombing.)

RAILROAD YARDS AT FOGGIA, ITALY
July 22, 1943

Railroad yards are prime targets for bombers. They represent a temporary concentration of food, ammunition, general supplies and fuel for the enemy's troops. On July 22, 1943, we made a raid on the Foggia railroad yards. This was our first journey to Foggia, southeast of Rome and about twenty-five miles from the Adriatic Sea. At that distance, we were again beyond fighter escort.

The battle would shape up differently for the enemy, too. While our course took us south of Naples and out of range of some enemy fighter bases, pursuit planes did harass us fifty miles before reaching the coast, where they were free to land and refuel at any convenient base. All conditions favored the defenders.

(General Upthegrove, in a letter written to me dated October 4, 1970, stated Hunter's top turret gunner, Sergeant Titus, was blown into the air with his parachute half buckled. He was taken prisoner. While being transferred by train, he escaped at the Brenner Pass. Somehow, he made his way south, got around the front lines by rafting and swimming the Adriatic and walked into British hands. They returned him to his group. (Sergeant Titus had quite a story to tell.)

Our gunners were kept busy as the enemy fighters relentlessly pressed their attack. Our loss taught us a bitter lesson and we resolved to do something about the situation.

We returned again, on August 19; this time to strike at the numerous anti-aircraft batteries which encircled the city. Having accomplished that task, we returned six days later, intent on knocking out the air base at Foggia. Once again, we met maximum opposition. It was my 32nd mission and the prospect of surviving 18 more weighed heavily on my mind.

With the invasion of Sicily behind us, the enemy was determined to stop our steady penetration. It was my duty, as co-pilot, to direct the gunners and scan the sky for enemy fighters. The target, Foggia, always brought murmurs of apprehension at the briefing after the first mission. I was to return again on August 25 and September 7. Other missions were flown by alternate crews when our crew was not scheduled.

On one of the missions, I spotted about a dozen fighters sitting out of range of our guns. I ordered my engineer, James Florek, in the upper turret, to begin firing. I wanted to let the enemy know we had them in our sight. "Lieutenant," he said over the intercom, "I want them to get in closer." "Give them a few tracers to let them know you mean business," I replied. While we were on the intercom, the fighters made a left turn-in-trail (they had a leader and each plane fell behind another) and zeroed in on our group with wing and cannon guns blazing.

ISERNIA, ITALY AND FROSINONE AIRDROME SEPTEMBER 5,1943

After Foggia, it was time for a breather; the briefing for the railroad bridges at Isernia was one of them. Perhaps the enemy considered them not important enough to protect. I made no notes or comments in my log.

The Frosinone mission to bomb the airdrome had some significance to me. It was my parents hometown. My maternal grandfather had a garment factory there in the 1930's. After his death, my mother's inheritance enabled her and my Dad to pay off the family farm mortgage - an opportunity not many had during the Depression.

Enemy fighters gave no opposition at Frosinone. We were forty miles north of Rome. Had we appeared on their radar, heading for the coast of Italy, it was a sure bet they would have been ready to protect their Capitol, Rome.

The Viterbo Airdrome raid by our group had no special memory for me. My entry was brief:

Viterbo A/D, 6 hours and 30 minutes.

That date, however, had great significance to Squadron Commander Harry Burrell. His ship was attacked by enemy fighters, whose fire wounded two crewmen seriously, frayed control cables, knocked out the radio equipment and damaged the landing flaps. He managed to get away from the fighters - while his gunners blasted down three - and landed safely in Sicily, where his wounded could be attended to. Harry was awarded the Silver Star for his gallantry in action on this mission.

COPY

HEADQUARTERS FIFTEENTH AIR FORCE G/UPD/res
APO 520 US Army

16 February 1944

GENERAL ORDERS)

NUMBER 50)

SECTION 1— AWARDS OF THE SILVER STAR

Under the provision of AR 600-45, as amended, and pursuant to authority contained in cable No. 9782, Headquarters NATOUS A, 5 December 1943, the Silver Star is awarded the following named personnel, residence and citation as indicated:

HARRY R. BURRELL, 0-387875, Major, Air Corps, United States Army. For gallantry in action as pilot of a B-17 type aircraft while participating in an important bombing mission over Viterbo Airdrome Italy, on 5 September 1943. Leading the second (2) wave toward the target, Major Burrell's ship was subjected to a head-on-attack by a formation of enemy fighters in a desperate attempt to scatter the bombing formation. Forced to lag momentarily from direct hits by 20 millimeter shells which wounded two (2) of his crew, disabled his controls, and damaged his radio system, Major Burrell gallantly and courageously held his course and led his formation through to the target, scoring direct hits on the objective and inflicting grave damage to the enemy. Unable to hold the formation after this gallant action, he then left his flight to allow them to proceed safely, and alone and unaided, managed to bring his damaged aircraft through enemy territory for a safe landing at a friendly base in Sicily. By his conspicuous gallantry and determination in carrying out his mission of leadership and great responsibility, regardless of all hazards, Major Burrell has reflected great credit upon himself and the Armed Forces of the United States of America. Residence at appointment: Omaha, Nebraska.

By command of Major General Twining.

Y. H. Taylor,
Colonel, GSC
Chief of Staff
OFFICIAL:

s/t J.M. Ivins,
Lieutenant Colonel, AGD
Adjutant General.
A TRUE COPY
W. V. McGarity (signed)

OVERRULED BY THE CO-PILOT

On September 10, 1943, I was given the privilege to fly the B-17 as First pilot. The co-pilot, whose plane I was flying, was one of the replacement First pilots. We had not gotten acquainted with each other before he was told to relinquish his seat to me for the mission. It was an easy trip to a highway bridge near the east coast of Italy. With little time over land, fighters were seldom near the coastal area.

We were about one hour into the six hour round trip mission when the vacuum pump on number 3 engine went out, causing the loss of all instruments needed for instrument flying. I knew instinctively that in the afternoon when we would be on the return over the vast area of the Mediterranean, thunderheads normally formed and much turbulence could be expected. I was assigned to fly in Bankhead's flight and was off his right wing. When the instruments went out, I had only the magnetic compass to rely on. It would deviate fifteen to thirty degrees in turbulent weather. I motioned to my co-pilot that we should drop out of formation and return to base because of the loss of the vacuum pump. He would not hear of it, and indicated we had to continue the mission. In my thirty—eight previous missions, I remembered many storms that would spring up during the afternoon while returning from Italian targets. Since it was the co-pilot's plane, I had no authority to overrule him. Even though it was presented to the briefing officer as an easy mission, I saw no reason to chance it without blind flying instruments.

We got to the target without opposition and began our return to Africa. We could already see clouds building up ahead of our return route. As the clouds became heavier and too difficult to keep a formation inside the storm clouds, the colonel radioed the group to loosen the formation and fly solo on our heading. Without my gyro compass that could keep me on a steady heading, I was forced to fly on Bankhead's right wing so I could keep the wings level and direction along with his plane. The heavy rain made the job very trying and dangerous. Suddenly, the turbulence within the thunderhead threw us out of formation. Inside the blackness we frantically looked for Bankhead's plane. At one hundred sixty miles per hour, we did not want a collision! Looking down the left side and some twenty feet below me, I spotted Bankhead's plane. It was too close and my first instinct was to go FULL THROTTLE and peel off to the right. The roar of our four engines startled Bankhead's crew who thought we were about to collide. All twenty men in those two B-17's breathed a lot easier after a close call! We could not afford to lose a single plane and the several hundred thousand dollars they cost to build. The war had a long way to go before the German war machine could be dealt the crippling blow.

CAIRO, EGYPT VISIT
SEPTEMBER 17, 1943

Our crew received a four day leave on September 17, together with some of our ground personnel to visit Cairo. We flew by way of Bengahsi, Libya viewing much of the battleground where Sir Bernard Montgomery, the greatest of Britain's Generals, fought the desert battles which finally saw the British Army triumph over Field Marshall Erwin Rommel in North Africa.

The desert sands had already buried much of the destroyed and abandoned tanks, trucks and other equipment immobilized by the struggle. How a soldier could exist and still fight in the sunbaked and wind-swept desert is truly a tribute to those brave men whose courage and determination won them the ultimate victory on the continent.

It took seven and one-half hours flying time to see the fertile land along the Nile River and civilization again. On landing to the east at the Cairo Airport, we passed over the towering spires of the city of Heliopolis, with the runway built uncomfortably close to the city.

The Sheppard's Hotel was our first stop and we were fortunate to have good accommodations for the entire party. We tried to speak our best French to the native Egyptians, and to our surprise they answered in the best King's English. Being a British Colony, it was no wonder the language was well spoken.

The next day, while walking through an area of the city, we met General Cheeves and General Russell of the OSS When they learned we had come for a short visit they sent us to the U.S. Army motor pool and had one of their captains accompany us to arrange for an American automobile to take a tour of the sights along the Nile. We thanked them graciously for their thoughtfulness and toured in a station wagon for the next two days.

It was suggested we hire a guide for the tour, and a kindly Egyptian named Ahmed agreed to do the honors for a fee of $20 which we divided among the six of us. The visits to the Pyramids and through the tombs of the ancient Egyptian Kings were impressive.

The men wanted to spend the rest of the war in Cairo but it was time to end the wonderful weekend. The shops had many beautiful gifts and trinkets that were masterfully handcrafted with hand made tools. A fine carved elephant that was reasonably priced for $3.50 and worth much more, must have taken dozens of hours of tedious labor to carve such minute details.

Back to the base. Our next mission, number 42 for the crew, on September 28, 1943, was to Bologna, Italy. That mission took us deep into Northern Italy and many hours over enemy territory. Our target was the railroad yards. Surprisingly, the fighter opposition and anti-aircraft fire was light; no planes were lost.

CHAPTER 9

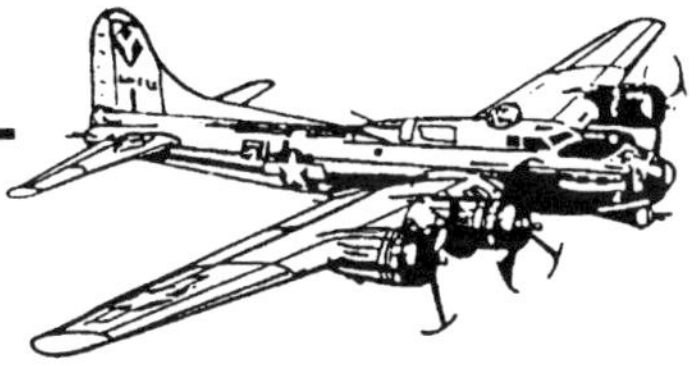

Terni And Weiner Neustadt

CAPTAIN BANKHEAD LEADS THE 347TH SQUADRON

October 21, 1943, Captain Bankhead and I had the honor of a nine ship mission to bomb the rail yards at Terni, Italy. Bankhead had been groomed to lead the new crews on bombing missions. He had ten more missions before he was to reach the total of 50. For myself, I had three more missions left for my 50th. All eight of our other planes were new crews who had some three to eight missions completed. For myself, I had the dreaded mission of 12 hours deep into Wiener Neustadt, Austria, Genoa, Italy and another viaduct on the Italian Riviera. I had no inkling these were extremely difficult missions.

Pope Laffoon and Bob Hain had worked their way up to element leaders and we were happy to have them on our squadron. We were on what was called a "maximum effort" mission as our usual complement was six ships per squadron.

It was a seven hour and ten minute trip from our base near Tunis, a base on the northern tip of the African Coast. We were not stationed at the base where we landed the crippled B-17 back on May 25, 1943. A larger base was needed for the "heavies" we flew.

Laffoon had the distinction of having a date with actress, Anna Lee, when she made a visit with Adolph Menjou at our base. After the program, I visited and talked to Menjou, with Anna Lee. I secured Menjou's signature on my "Short Snorter" (a dollar bill signed by those who had crossed the ocean).

We never did know where in the African town of Navarin some ten miles away they could find a suitable Arab restaurant or club. Anna Lee was told before she left the States to look up Pope when she got to Africa. We were happy for him as he was one fine Air Corps pilot.

WEINER NEUSTADT AUSTRIA MISSION, OCTOBER 24, 1943

On October 24th, we were briefed on another deep penetration into enemy territory. The target was the ball bearing factory at Wiener Neustadt, Austria. There was a stir among the pilots, the navigators and the bombardiers when the mission was disclosed by the briefing officer.

The wall map charted our course from Tunis in North Africa to Grottagglie Air Base in Tarranto, Italy. We would be flying a direct route to the toe of Italy through the very heart of Sicily, the Sicily we had feared to enter only a few months before. The airdromes were no longer a threat. Gerbini Airdrome had lost its fighter planes, 51 in our July 5th mission. Messina was no longer in the hands of the German Army. On this trip we could enjoy a few hours of quiet scenery. Guns were silenced in the five months our bomber groups pounded the island. And Palermo! How could we ever forget it?!

We stayed at the base overnight and took off the next morning, heading north up the Adriatic Sea and entered Yugoslavia near the city of Belgrade. Our route took us directly over Zagreb, the capital of Yugoslavia, and 150 miles north was our target, the ball bearing factory complex.

To destroy this target was to deny the German Air Force the bail bearings needed for their bombers and fighters. There was no question the mission was vital.

Unlike the Messina, Sicily mission, our gunners did not jump at the prospect of this mission. Being over enemy land areas for hundreds of miles with the chance of exhausting ammunition from repeated fighter attacks was a constant worry to them. Also, our right waist gunner, Frank Kovac, was ill that day and they were apprehensive about the gunner assigned to replace him. We proceeded as scheduled and arrived for our overnight stay at Grottagglie Air Base.

We were allowed off the base that evening and our crew went to the city of Tarranto for our evening dinner. I could speak Italian quite fluently and we talked to a man at a street corner about dinner for our group of six people. He asked us if we would be willing to enjoy some of his wife's cooking which, of course, we accepted after agreeing on the price of the meal.

You can imagine our surprise upon arriving at his modest abode to find he also had four lovely daughters. I had not planned it, but I had several packages of Camel and Lucky Strike cigarettes and several packages of gum with me. The eyebrows of the father and daughters went up a few inches and the smiles lightened up the room as I brought out my coveted cache. Who could concentrate on food with the four lovely daughters doting on us? Our eyes were upon them, one lovelier than the other. Had we been away too long?

In these pleasant surroundings, we forgot for the moment, our concern over the next day's mission. For a few hours, we were joking and enjoying ourselves with our host. They had never seen American airmen and expressed relief at being rid of the Germans.

Our dinner consisted of soup, chicken and fish. You can imagine the many loving glances cast upon those lovely girls as they helped "Papa" with serving. "Mama" cooked a fine meal and dedicated her efforts in the kitchen. Later, she talked with me about my mother and father and was surprised to learn they grew up near Rome, Italy.

I told them I was on my forty-eighth mission and would soon be going home. They wished us well and hoped the war would be over soon.

The next morning our three groups took off to complete the mission. All the men tried to put on a bold front, but within them they knew of the danger that lay ahead.

It was our first foray deep into the nest of German opposition. Until now it had been our counterparts, the Eighth Air Force out of England, who had the task of enduring the heavy flack and swarms of German fighters. Flying that deep into enemy territory and the tours over their region was not what we had been accustomed to. Striking seaport targets and a quick escape over water was less stressful. Enemy fighters had little fuel left after they challenged the bombers over the target. They had to turn back to the coast and their airfield before exhausting their fuel. On this trip, they had a plentiful supply of bases in Yugoslavia and Austria to find refuge. They were able to stay up and harass us much longer. There was the possibility our gunners could run out of ammunition if a protracted battle became necessary.

The flight over the Adriatic Sea was a beautiful sight. We crossed the Yugoslav coastline at an altitude of 10,000 feet seeing patches of brown clay on the plowed fields below. A lone burst of flak greeted us in the vicinity of the capital of Zagreb. We were now about 140 miles from the target and our gunners were instructed to check their guns to make sure they were not freezing at this high altitude.

Our tail gunner excitedly called us on the interphone and told us our horizontal stabilizer was shot full of holes. It turned out the replacement gunner, while testing his waist guns, had pointed them downward. Each burst had caused the .50 caliber gun to progress upward until he cut through the stabilizer. His excuse for not firing toward the sky was that he wanted to avoid the P-38 fighter escort above us.

The prospect of going into a zone of heavy fighter opposition with a weakened tail section gave us no choice but to think of the safety of the crew so Captain Bankhead made the decision to return to the Grottagglie Air Base. We were relieved to turn back, but the manner in which we had to turn back was embarrassing.

Our eyes were glued to the horizon about 3:00 P.M. when our planes were due back. We counted the planes in each squadron as they neared the field and breathed a sigh of relief to see they had all returned safely.

After all planes were parked on the field, we learned the group commander found the target overcast. He decided not to drop the bomb load, even though the IP (initial point) was visible.

The initial point was located about ten miles away and could be seen through the overcast. One thing we were certain of: that mission would be re-scheduled and this time the fighters would be there waiting for us.

Photo: Courtesy of General Upthegrove

I was long gone when the Group began the missions into Austria and others closer to Germany.

Note the three B-17's down low, relative to the one up high with bomb bay doors still open.

347th SQUADRON FORMATION

MISSION OCTOBER 21, 1943

347th TWINDYKE

Bankhead-G
705

Ossori-T
339

Campbell-C
462

Laffoon-G
818

Ray-D
389

Pixler-J
490

Hain-B
164

Dodge-K
473

Wardwell-N
769

CHAPTER 10

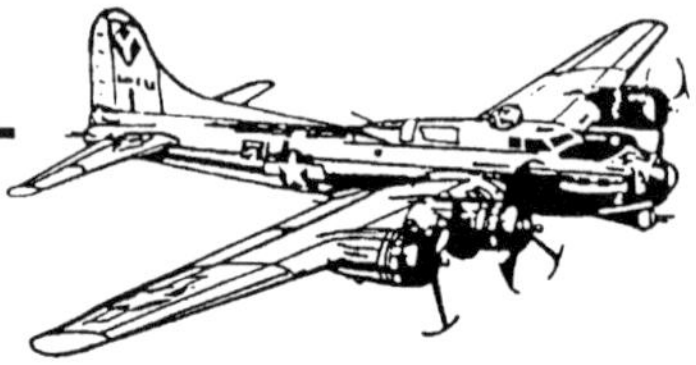

THE 49TH AND 50TH MISSIONS

October 29th another mission which is still fresh and vivid in my memory. This should be the time for me to be relieved of most of the dangers of being an American aerial combatant was close at hand; however, I was still apprehensive about reaching 50 missions alive.

What we had known all along was that direct burst by anti-aircraft fire or from an enemy fighter into the gas tank or bomb bay area could prove fatal and severely cripple the bomber and crew. I was always hoping and praying this would not happen to any of us.

Our mission on this day was to strike the railroad yards at Genoa, Italy. It was a seven hour and ten minute round trip, with more than seven hours being over the north-south expanse of the Mediterranean Sea. Our group was the third to hit the target. As we were approaching the coast of Italy and still some ten miles over water we saw a B-17 ahead of us on a bomb run explode into a red ball of fire. Either a gas tank received a direct hit, or a bomb fuse could have been hit by shrapnel and triggered the entire bomb load. No one gave a report and we saw no parachutes coming out of the burning inferno.

I was flying co-pilot for Captain Clark, who had almost as many missions to his credit as I did. We looked at each other and knew not one of the crewmen could have survived the explosion. We silently prayed. We continued on to the target, hoping against hope the enemy would not be able to send up two deadly accurate bursts in one day. They did have our range and altitude. The plane hit was directly ahead of us at the same altitude.

Even as we dropped our bomb on the tracks and freight yards, red-hot anti-aircraft fragments filled the air around us. That is a sight which makes anybody squirm! We were relieved when we could turn off of the target and head home. There was to be only one more adventure of this kind ahead for me.

Luckily, all of our squadron survived the barrage of bursting flack and made the diving turn away from the target after all bombs had cleared the bomb bays and the long journey back to Africa could be another satisfying escape from the uncertain fate. It was now time for me to look forward to my last and 50th mission.

THE LAST MISSION

My last mission came two days later on October 31, 1943. Again, I was slated to be Captain Clark's co-pilot. This time we led the second wave of our squadron.

The flight was a long one. The railroad viaduct on the coast of France, near the Italian Riviera, was much like the Genoa mission. This trip would be seven hours and twenty minutes in flying time. We were to knock out the Antheor railroad viaduct along the southern coast of France.

We were the lead group and a second group was to follow in trail after our run. The groups were on the bomb run with no fighter opposition and light anti-aircraft fire. I happened to glance upward as we headed down the bomb run at a heading of forty-five degrees. To my surprise, I watched in horror as the second bombing group was not following in trail, but had cut short their initial point and were making a run on the viaduct with bomb bay doors open directly above our squadron! Our bombardier was signaling Captain Clark to steer to the left in order to strike the target. I called attention to Captain Clark we were about to be bombed by the group above us who had gotten out of position and were heading to the viaduct at a heading nearer to twenty degrees. I continued motioning to the Captain to veer to the right, thereby ignoring the bombardier's position indicator to veer left. The Captain followed my suggestion. I felt our survival was more important than the viaduct. My reasoning was that with some 48 planes aiming for the railroad viaduct, our three planes were not crucial to the mission.

As our group began the three and one-half hour trip back to our base in Tunis, I was happily singing the tune, "Taking A Chance On Love" to myself. I had survived the 50th mission and a trip home to the United States was in sight.

Our planes were silhouetted against the usual storm bank of clouds. At that moment, the squadron photographer took a picture of our plane, "RANGY LIL" against the background of a beautiful rainbow. He presented it to me as a keepsake of the last mission out of Africa.

Author, James F. Bruno, 2nd Lieutenant.
50th Mission photo in front of Captain Clark's B-17

Photo from James F. Bruno Collection

"RANGY LIL" returning from Antheor railroad viaduct bombing mission. Plane was piloted by Captain William Clark.

This was the author's 50th and last combat mission in the North African theater.

THE 51st MISSION
VISIT THE FRENCH CAPTAIN'S WIFE!

I was enjoying the completion of my 50 missions and awaiting orders to return to the States. One of our gunners rushed into our officers' tent. "Lieutenant Bruno," he ordered, "will you hurry into Tunis, go to Room 22 of the hotel and tell Danielle I'm going on a dangerous mission inside of Germany and may not make it back."

Danielle was a French Captain's wife he met at a Tunis restaurant. Our gunner learned her husband was away "at the front" and "may not return." He believed it was his duty to rescue the "damsel in distress."

Now the shoe was on the other foot! Our man felt he might not return!

I was in good spirits having completed my 50 missions. Not so with my friend - he was going deep into the hornet's nest of the German Luftwaffe pilots!

I accepted his request to deliver the package of cigarettes to Danielle, as a token of his affection. Without divulging my destination, I checked out a Jeep at the motor pool. At the hotel, I walked hurriedly up the stairway and went directly to Room 22.

With a very light touch, I knocked on the door. From the other side of it her voice softly asked, "Who is there?" After identifying myself, I informed her I had a message from our gunner. Slowly, she opened the door.

For a moment, I stared; taken aback by the vision of a very beautiful lady with long, shining dark brown hair falling softly onto her shoulders. A brilliant red satin negligee flowed around her shapely body.

"Please come in," she said in her native language.

Tiny bare feet peeked out beneath the hem of her gown. She turned and directed me to follow her to the bed where she gently sat down and pointed to a place alongside her for me. As I did so, the heady scent of her exquisite French perfume wafted before me and brought back memories of Irene, when we danced together before the war. Her tousle headed two-year old son had awakened and was standing at the foot of the bed with the usual childish innocent stare.

In my very best French, I explained her friend's urgent message. Her radiant coal black eyes searched mine in understanding; then she said with an impassioned longing in her delightful voice, "He is such a magnificent man! I am going to miss him so very much!" In a composed voice, I agreed; my compatriot was "Quite a guy!"

Time stood still as we described how each of us became acquainted with this "fine gentleman." The spell was broken as she ripped open the pack of cigarettes and asked me for a light! Not being a smoker, I said I would go downstairs to the desk and obtain a pack of matches.

As I stepped into the hallway, I saw a man approaching. It was the Sergeant! "Man!" I called out, "am I glad to see you!" "Why are you here?" "The mission was scrubbed," he said, and strode hurriedly past me into Room 22.

My mission was completed! Happily, I drove back to the base to prepare for a return home.

The matches?! I'm certain my friends had their smoke together——much later!

347th BOMBARDMENT SQUADRON (H)
ARMY AIR FORCES
OFFICE OF THE OPERATIONS OFFICER

APO #620, NATOUSA,
31 October, 1943.

I CERTIFY that 2nd Lt BRUNO, JAMES F., ASN 0-729804, Pilot, has completed the following fifty (50) Operational Missions totaling 312 hours and 40 minutes:

Date	Mission No.	Target	Hours
3-31-43	1	Villacridro A/D, Sardinia	3:45
4-10-43	2	La Maddalena N/B, Sicily	5:55
4-11-43	3	Marsala, Sicily	4:50
4-12-43	4	Trapani, Sicily	2:10
4-17-43	5	Palermo, Sicily	5:45
4-20-43	6	Siddi Hamed A/D, No. Afr.	2:50
5-6-43	7	Marsala, Sicily	5:05
5-9-43	8	Palermo, Sicily	5:45
5-10-43	9	Milo A/D, Trapani	4:45
5-11-43	10	Marsala, Sicily	4:40
5-13-43	11	Caglieri, Sardinia	3:30
5-14-43	12	Civitavecchia	6:50
5-18-43	13	Trapani, Sicily	5:45
5-19-43	14	Sciacca, Sicily	4:30
5-21-43	15	Castelvetrano, Sicily	4:55
5-26-43	16	Messina, Sicily	7:00
6-15-43	17	Bocca Di Falco, Sicily	6:20
6-18-43	18	Messina, Sicily	8:00
6-25-43	19	Messina, Sicily	7:45
6-28-43	20	Leghorn, Italy	7:25
6-30-43	21	Palermo, Sicily	5:45
7-5-43	22	Gerbini, Sicily	6:50
7-12-43	23	Messina, Sicily	6:20

Date	Mission No.	Target	Hours
7-14-43	24	Messina, Sicily	6:35
7-15-43	25	Naples, Italy	6:50
7-19-43	26	Rome, Italy	7:00
7-21-43	27	Grosetto A/D, Italy	7:05
7-22-43	28	Foggia, Italy	7:55
7-24-43	29	Bologna, Italy	10:10
8-9-43	30	Messina, Sicily	4:10
8-17-43	31	Le Tube A/D, Marseille, France	7:15
8-19-43	32	Foggia, Italy	5:40
8-25-43	33	Foggia, Italy	5:35
9-2-43	34	Bologna, Italy	6:50
9-5-43	35	Viterbo, Italy	5:50
9-6-43	36	Naples, Italy	5:15
9-7-43	37	Foggia, Italy	6:25
9-9-43	38	Caugua, Italy	5:30
9-10-43	39	Isorne, Italy	5:30
9-12-43	40	Frosinone, Italy	5:25
9-16-43	41	Bonevento, Italy	5:35
9-28-43	42	Bologna, Italy	6:45
10-5-43	43	Bologna, Italy	7:25
10-6-43	44	Mestra, Italy	8:35
10-9-43	45	Salonika A/D, Greece	9:05
10-14-43	46	Terni, Italy	6:10
10-21-43	47	Terni, Italy	6:45
10-24-43	48	Wiener Neustadt, Austria	12:00
10-29-43	49	Genoa, Italy	7:35
10-31-43	50	Antheor RRV, Italy	7:20
			312:40

HEBER B. BANKHEAD,
Captain, Air Corps,
Operations Officer.

CHAPTER 11

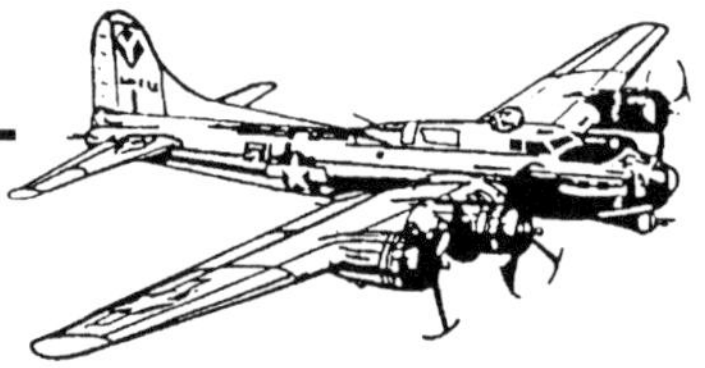

THE GI'S VS THE ARAB GYPSIES

(Reprinted with permission of the Milwaukee Journal)

Veterans of the North African Campaign Can't Forget the Wily Tribesman Who Gave Them Some Trouble and No End of Amusement

The North African invasion on November 8, 1942, marked the opening of the "Second Front," but more memorable for the participating American GI's, it marked the beginning of their acquaintance with the Arabs.

Many unpleasant memories of that campaign - the dust, the heat, the flies, the bitter cold of the desert at night may fade with time, but not the soldier's recollection of his dealings with the dark skinned natives of French northwest Africa. However, the dictionaries and the encyclopedias designate these peoples, to the every day American soldier they were "A-rabs".

Statistics may make much of UNRRA aid to French North Africa, but any soldier who served there will maintain that it was unnecessary. The GI's contend some of the native population should be able to live comfortably for at least the next decade on what they begged, bartered and "borrowed" from the liberating armies.

One victim of unofficial lend-lease was an American officer courier who, when billeted overnight in an Algiers hotel, made the mistake of removing his trousers for sleeping. Dead tired from a grueling drive from the front in Tunisia, and wanting to make the most of the unaccustomed good fortune of a bed, he undressed before dropping exhausted into its soft folds. His upstairs room, being on the downhill side of the building, was a good three stories above the winding, cobbled street; yet, he awoke to find his trousers, wallet and all missing. Sheepishly, he sought our a supply dump next morning, attired in battle dress complete to a helmet and combat boots, but minus his pants. He never forgave the Gypsy "human fly" who had humiliated him, nor did his friends ever permit the incident to be forgotten.

A mechanized cavalry troop patrolling the border between Spanish and French Morocco, shortly after the invasion, bivouacked in a cork forest near the village of Ain Defali. Following army directives that an attitude of friendliness be exhibited toward the natives, the troop commander permitted a number of Gypsies to wander through the camp accepting proffered cigarettes, candy and "C" rations. At the edge of the grove a small tribe of the sultan's subjects squatted and stared.

Mess call sounded and the soldiers who were pitching pup tents for the night ran for the chow line, leaving their equipment and extra clothing scattered about. They neglected to post a guard. Returning to their tasks after finishing their warmed up cans of hash, the troopers found their tents surprisingly barren. A group of heavily burdened Gypsies was seen vanishing into the grove.

Only two of the culprits were overtaken, one of them an old man whose speed was handicapped by age. The other was a young man, but he was carrying too much. Beneath his robe were enough parts of uniforms to outfit half a squad of men. Even so, he might have outdistanced his pursuers had he not attempted to include two boxes of machine gun ammunition. The weight handicap was too much, and he lost the race.

In North Africa more than one American soldier was to learn from bitter experience the consequences of tanking up on too much wine. A luckless GI making his unsteady way toward barracks one night was held up by three Gypsy youths and relieved of his clothing to the last stitch. He reported to the nearest MP station clad only in his socks. With a borrowed raincoat and under escort, he made his way to camp, a chilled but sober and wiser man.

On another occasion, a mess officer on his way to the commissary with the day's receipts was seized on either side by two Gypsy thugs who ripped both front pockets away and made off with the mess fund. After a short sprint, the two "highwaymen" disappeared into the labyrinth of the Algiers Casbah along with the $500 in Francs.

A soldier, left behind in the desert to guard his unit's surplus baggage, found himself constantly surrounded by a silent circle of squatting Gypsies. Each time he dozed, a duffel bag disappeared. Awaking each morning, he discovered that the pile had grown smaller during the night. Obviously, drastic action was necessary, or he would have nothing left to guard, the sentry reasoned.

That night, as a Gypsy was about to make off with a duffel bag, the soldier shot him in his tracks and buried the corpse in a shallow grave. Next morning a group of natives spying the mound and thinking it was a garbage pit they had not previously excavated, began to dig. Suddenly they uncovered the body of their comrade. Pandemonium followed the gruesome discovery. There were no more duffel bags stolen!

Members of the 12th air service command, which had its headquarters in the Algerian capital, will never forget Abdul

K. lsker, one of the most artful "feather merchants" to come out of the war. "Feather merchant" was the Gl term for a black marketeer deluxe, a nefarious schemer.

A denizen of the Algiers Casbah, Abdul was a born swindler. Over a period of six months he gained considerable notoriety through his relations with, first the Germans, for whose armistice commission he worked, and later with the Americans and British. Strictly neutral, he stole from them all. Despite his origin, Abdul acquired a considerable degree of polish through studious application at the University of Algiers, and spoke flawless French and Oxford English. Outwardly, a suave gentleman, he was an accomplished rogue.

Abdul promptly attached himself to American headquarters as an interpreter following the hasty departure of his German masters. In no time he was hiring and firing all native help. He enjoyed a fabulous income from the tribute paid by the Arab laborers to get on and stay on the payroll The workers stole everything they could lay their hands on, turning over most of the swag to Abdul, who disposed of it in the black market. During his tenure, the flow of supplies to the battle front ebbed noticeably.

There is no record that Abdul's hirelings ever "lifted" a tank or a plane, but; unquestionably, several of either kind of machine could have been assembled from the spare parts they pilfered. At length, as most criminals do, Abdul K. Isker grew careless and the Tommies caught him red handed. After a speedy trial he was incarcerated in one of the foulest colonial prisons deep in the Algerian desert.

Few of his former friends believed that any jail could contain the ingenious Abdul. By this time, they insisted, Abdul had established himself respectfully in Algiers as a merchant dealing in "surplus" army supplies.

* * *

American troops knew little about inflation when they sailed from home early in the autumn of 1942, but they were soon to feel its effects in North Africa. Within a few days, the "price" of eggs advanced from one package of cigarettes for a dozen to one package for a single egg.

The persistently shrewd Arab trader never displayed all his wares, and regardless of whatever item competing soldiers might be bidding for, it was never the last. From the inner recesses of his long, hooded burnoose, the native could always produce "just one more", be it a goat or a basket of eggs. From the mysterious folds of his robe, one Arab pulled a half bushel of citrus fruit, four chickens and six baskets of eggs. In all probability, as an onlooking soldier remarked, he held a couple of hand woven rugs in reserve.

* * *

When the 99th Bomb Group moved to the airfield at Djeideida, near Tunis, it was welcomed by a motley delegation of Arab tradesmen headed by Mohammed H. Muhatanat, who bartered in three languages. Mohammed offered eggs at 25 cents apiece.

A combat camera man proposed that a contract be negotiated where Mohammed would supply a dozen and a half eggs daily, in return for which he would become the owner of a sleek Flying Fortress. After careful scrutiny of one of the four engined giants, the Arab agreed. To seal the bargain, Mohammed's name was inscribed boldly on the tail of one of the newer B-17's.

Following his daily delivery of the prescribed count of eggs, the Moslem trader would walk around his private airship, regarding it with a satisfied gleam. Occasionally, he would run his hand over its glistening surfaces. On his way home through the camp, Mohammed picked up whatever happened to be lying around. On one occasion it happened to be the complete baggage set of the unit chaplain.

Late in August, 1943, Mohammed observed unusual activity at the field. Trucks were darting about and planes were being loaded with equipment not ordinarily taken on routine flights. However, he did not dwell upon it, for had not M. le Caporal personally assured him that the plane would be his in a very few days?

As he watched, the Flying Fortress bearing Mohammed's name rose majestically from the far end of the field to disappear in the haze high over the Gulf of Tunis. It was the last time Mohammed ever saw his "great white bird" or his 45 dozen eggs.

CHAPTER 12

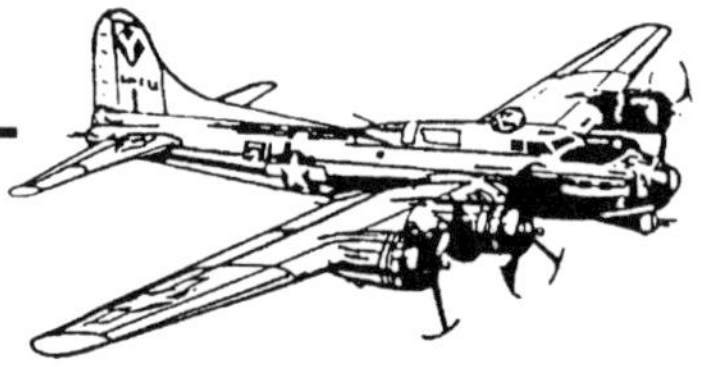

THE 99TH BOMBARDMENT GROUP CELEBRATES THE FIRST 100 BOMBING MISSIONS

Major Harry Burrell had the honor of leading the group on its 100th mission. As Harry taxied to a stop, he was greeted by Group Commander, Colonel Fay R. Upthegrove. The Colonel had already completed his 50 missions and was slated to go home for a period of rest before returning to combat.

Before the assembled men of the 99th and the generals and other high ranking Army officers, Colonel Upthegrove gave this history and praise to the men he had commanded for the past 14 months:

"Beginning September 15, 1942, Boise, Idaho - fought for a cadre, assigned in orders dated September 25 and moved to Walla Walla, Washington on September 30. During October our cadre was augmented until we were nearly at top strength. That month we had 4 planes and 4 model crews. October 20, we received our flight commanders and on November 1, 36 combat crews and a total of twelve aircraft. Immediately, the training grind started 24 hours a day. The weather forced us out of Walla Walla two weeks early and we moved to Sioux City, Iowa. There, between snow squalls, we completed our training by the end of December and were pronounced ready to proceed to Salina, Kansas for final check and staging prior to departure overseas.

One crew was lost in training. We picked up 35 new B-17's at Salina and checked our equipment. Meanwhile, due to lack of shipping, our ground echelon was staged at Watertown, North Dakota and Mitchell, South Dakota. The combat crews augmented by staff members and other key personnel departed Salina on January 18, again due to weather, completing our navigational and radio checks at De Ridder, Louisiana.

On January 31, we shoved on to Morrison Field at West Palm Beach for another final processing and clearance overseas. The flight echelon was split in half, spaced a day apart, and on the mornings of February 3rd and 4th, 1943, our great adventure began. Our orders were to England. Except for a few stragglers we arrived at Marrakech on February 10th and 12th, having lost one day in Puerto Rico due to weather. For two nights we were unable to clear for England due to weather and on February 13th we received a hold order signed SPAATZ. We were all quite pleased and eagerly awaited confirmation of our assignment to the North African Theater. It came a couple of days later and after further delay due to weather we proceeded to La Senia, Oran for airplane check up and flight and ground training by the training command. We were there approximately one month and moved forward to Chateau Dun on March 23rd and 24th. Split between the 97th and 301st for a couple of days we moved as quickly as possible to our own field at Navarin.

With about 100 men loaned by the 301st and 97th Bomb Groups and the help of the Service Squadron at Navarin, we declared ourselves operational and flew our first mission on March 31st. We were not to see our ground echelon for almost two months. Meanwhile they had their troubles, too. Rumor had it that we were going to lose them and they were sent to Oklahoma City to help processing out for a month. Then to Camp Kilmer and at long last, very impatient, embarked for overseas and landed at Oran. In due time, after gathering together most of our equipment, they jolted up to Navarin on the French Railroad Express arriving on May 25th. Once again we were united and everyone was happy. We, to see our own people, and the old groups to get their loaned personnel back.

Those two months were very trying and I cannot pay too high a tribute to the faithful and outstanding assistance these borrowed personnel rendered; without them we could not have functioned at all. Since that time we have plugged away at the job of axing the axis, and with no intent to boast, feel that we have done a fine job and more than justified our existence. Only a few members of our original crews are left. New arrivals were welcomed into the fold and soon were pulling their share and I'm confident will continue to do so as long as the group shall live. Our morale is still high and I want to pay particular tribute to our staff and ground personnel for the loyal, willing and untiring efforts put forth, mainly without much hope of glory or reward. They are the backbone of the group and our success is theirs. Teamwork here is the key to success and I cannot reiterate enough how grateful and proud we combat people are of each and everyone from K.P. to Executive Officer. The commanding officer does not make the group - all of you collectively make the group. Its success or failure, past, present and future, are in your hands.

We claim no special distinction in our record and have had our ups and downs. During the first 100 missions we have dropped 12,956,320 pounds of bombs on a score of targets. Of 1028 aircraft encountered, we have destroyed 259, probably destroyed 64 and damaged at least 60. We have destroyed 466 on the ground. Other damage to the enemy's shipping and installations is beyond price.

Regrettably and inevitably we have had losses, 19 killed in action, 69 wounded and 99 missing from 11 crews. Many of those missing are alive but prisoners of war. We will not forget them for they were our buddies and among our favorite people. We can, however, continue to be worthy of their sacrifice.

Battle flights have taken us over the snow capped Alps, the jagged peaks of Corsica, the leaning Tower of Pisa, the Vatican City in Rome, the smoking cones of Mt Vesuvius and Etna, Ancient Athens, the French Riviera, the vineyards of Italy, the olive groves of Sardinia, the Roman Aqueduct in North Africa and many other historic places. We have touched the heights at times and participated in the two biggest bomber pursuit battles of this theater. We more than held our own. 59 members have had to bail out for various reasons and we have our own "Silk Crackers Club". We have our individual and collective heroes and have earned numerous awards both in the air and on the ground. Our photo section has made 2,414 negatives and 18,491 prints of aerial shots and 820 pictures with 6369 prints of ground shots for press release and historical data. Those are some of the things which has kept us busy for the past seven months.

Time will bring changes in personnel, equipment and location. We cannot stagnate or stand still. The spirit of the Fighting 99th will live, however, through you and those to follow.

May I again express my sincere appreciation to every member of the group for your faithful service and loyalty, to our senior commanders and staffs for their wise counsel, to our allied service personnel for their cooperation and understanding and to the American Red Cross for coffee and doughnuts.

In case you had doubts, I am going to stop now and introduce our distinguished guests.

Colonel Rogers - Graduate of Wright Field Engineering School with years of experience in the intricate science of keeping them flying. Present head of 2nd SAC his job is to keep us supplied with all the necessities of living as well as fighting. He holds a very tough job and an important one. Don't bet that he can't do the job and don't bet against him on the golf course.

United States Army Air Force - North African Commanders at the 99th Bomb Group 100 Mission Celebration.

Left to right: **Lieut. Gen. Carl Spaatz, Brig. Gen. Jimmy Doolittle, Col. Fay R. Upthegrove, 99th Commander, Brig. Gen. Lauris Norstad, Brig. Gen. Earle Partridge, and Col. Norme Frost.**

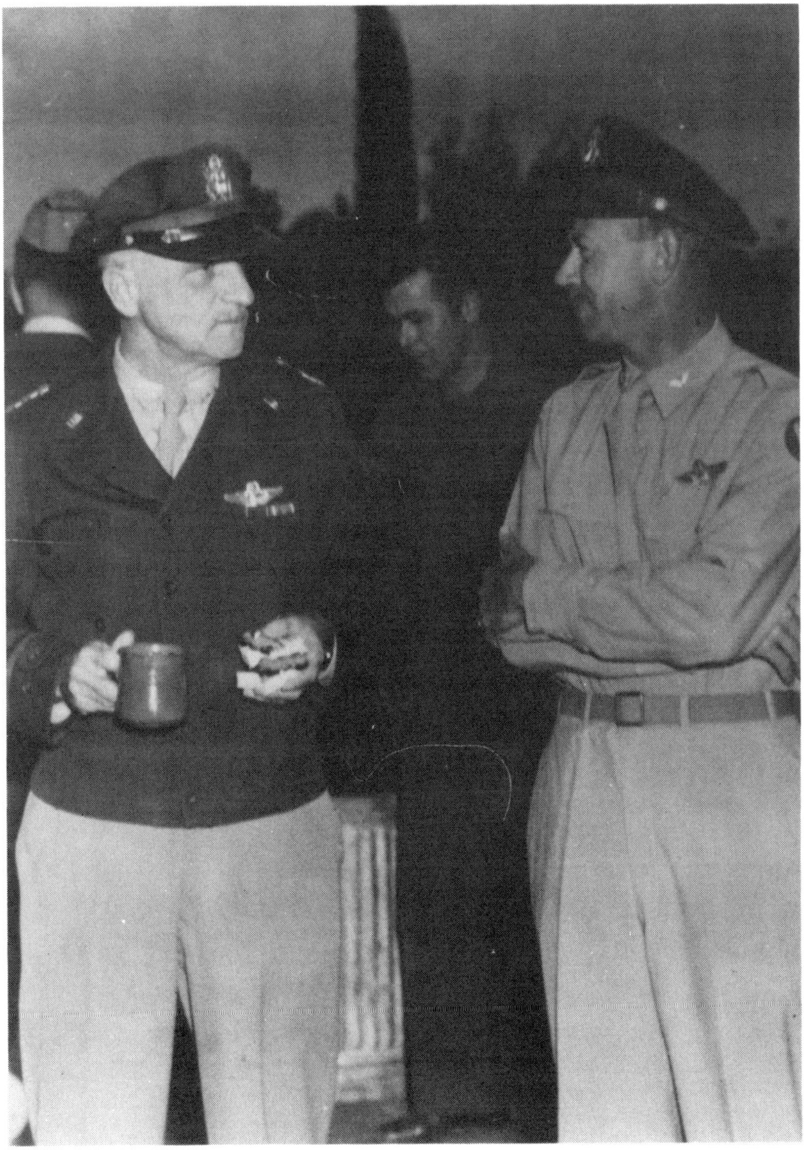

99th Bomb Group 100th Mission Celebration
Lt. General Carl Spaatz with Col. Fay R. Upthegrove.

Col. F. R. Upthegrove greets Maj. Harry R. Burrell just returned from the 100th mission of the 99th.
This was also Harry's 50th.

General Bartron - Chief ASAC. One of the senior officers in the Air Corps whose specialty for many years has been supply. In 1931, he established and ran the Air Corps Supply at Randolph Field, the newly established "West Point of the Air" and has been hammering away at it ever since.

Colonel Frost - Wing CO in General Atkinson's absence. A pursuit pilot first, then an instructor for a time he turned to communications and spent several years at Chanute Field perfecting ways and means of licking that every present bugaboo, "vocal contact".

B. General Born - All American end at West Point after a few years in the cavalry, found out a horse couldn't fly and joined the Air Corps. At present holding the very important post of A-3 of Strategic Air Force, he is one of the experts whose chess moves will soon spell "checkmate" to the Axis.

General Norstad - West Point Class of 1930 - one of our youngest generals - will now hold the very important post of A-3 in charge of operations of the combined American and British Air Forces in this theater. He participated in the planning and execution of the landing in North Africa and is still in there pitching, conjuring up new pinpricks with which to puncture the propaganda balloons of Herr Goebbels & Co.

General Doolittle - Ever since I can remember it has been generally acknowledged that Jimmy Doolitte has been America's foremost flier. In the Army for many years, he resigned for a time to conduct experiments to further the progress of aviation. With the United States in trouble, he promptly came back, scared the hell out of the Japs in Tokyo and has since settled down to the fine art of repeatedly heckling the hun. How well he is doing that is well known to all of us who have in a small measure been able to help.

General Spaatz - You all know the last distinguished General. One of the very early pioneers of Army Aviation he has been a part of the stubborn growth of the Air Corps since its conception. He saw active aerial combat in the last war and has observed the transition from that "Sporting Stage as it were to the highly deadly and scientific destructive force which we are gradually building up to unleash on the foe in this one. He has spent more years in aviation than most of you have lived. It give me the keenest pleasure to introduce our own supreme American Air Commander, General Spaatz.

CHAPTER 13

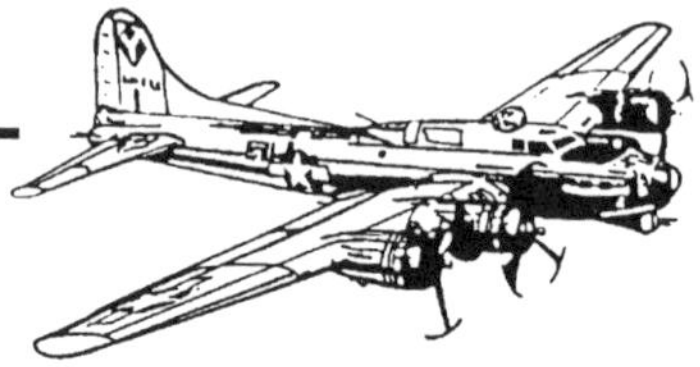

THE 300 MISSION LOG

THE 99th BOMB GROUP REACHES 300th MISSION

Most members of the original 99th who went overseas in February, 1943 were in the States at new assignments when the Group celebrated Mission Number 300. They even had their own newspaper. Here, through the courtesy of General Upthegrove, are excerpts of that fine publication:

99th BOMB GROUP THREE HUNDRED MISSION LOG

Published on the occasion of the Three-hundredth Combat Mission flown in the Mediterranean Theater of Operations by the air crews of the 99th Bombardment Group (H), Army Air Forces; Ford J. Lauer, Colonel, Air Corps, Commanding.

Editorial Staff	1st Lt. Harold J. Blum, Sgt. John R.Wiggin
Art Staff	Major John W. Huflon, S-Sgt Leo V. Anderson
Photo Staff	T-Sgt. Eugene F. Sullivan and Group photo Section

LEAST WE FORGET

Chaplain Harold T Whitlock

Two years ago we suffered our first fatality in the Group. The shock of that crew's death was deeply felt. How fortunate we were that only one crew was lost in training. And our good fortune has continued throughout nineteen months of combat flying. Losses by death have been remarkably low.

It is right that we should pause in this, our proud celebration, to think for a moment and to say a prayer for those friends who have not come back and of those who have flown their final mission.

When they got up at "H" hour on that fatal day there was nothing that marked them apart from the others on the loading list. They were ordinary fellows like the rest of them, the kind of men we used to see at ball games and fairs, or in offices, shops and churches. Men from all walks of life, of all classes of society, from every section of our land. Some were tousle-haired youngsters not yet matured by combat; others were seasoned veterans of many missions over unfriendly territory. Not one of them wanted to die - they had too much to live for, each has his particular hopes for the future. But they were men in a dangerous business, trained to do a needed and important job, and willing to risk themselves to accomplish their mission. They were expendable - they knew it - and some were spent.

Someone will speak of them as having "lost their lives," but was it so? They were in a fight to protect and perpetuate things worth more than life, things without "which life could not be worth living. "Tis man's perdition to be safe, when for the truth he ought to die." To that great cause they had given fully of their time, their thought, their skill, their energy. Can it then be said they did not give their lives as well?

No life laid down in a great cause is ever wasted. It lives on in the ideal they died to maintain. If their sacrifice means anything at all, it means that we, the living, must rededicate ourselves to the future for which they died. The man who can remember them, and then breathe easily and say, "Let's get back to our former ways; things can go on as before,: is a traitor to his times and to them. Things must not go on as before. Their giving must not have been in vain. The world which we build will be their monument."

So let us pause and pray: "Oh God, to all who bravely laid down their lives, grant perfect peace; shelter them forever under the cover of thy wings; and in thy loving wisdom and almighty power work through them and us the purposes of thy good and holy will, that men may live in peace on earth and evermore, Amen."

VETERAN FORT GROUP LOGS 300 MISSIONS

Catching the rays of the late afternoon sunlight, on November 20, 1944, 36 B-17s of the 99th Bomb Group peeled off and landed at their Italian base. The great, silver Flying Fortresses, led that day by Major Wayne J. Seward, Commanding Officer of the 416th Squadron had just completed the 99th's three hundredth mission.

As Major Seward dropped through the nose hatch of his ship, after parking it in its revetment, he was warmly greeted by Colonel Ford J. Lauer, the Group Commander. Cameras clicked, and congratulations were extended to the men who had flown that day. In the background the ever-presented ground crews were already servicing the bombers for the next day's operations. Before the flying personnel had finished gathering their gear, mechanics and armorers and communications men were making their careful checks of equipment, and the huge tank trucks were gassing up the almost empty tanks of the aircraft.

Target for the historic mission was the marshalling yards at Brno, Czechoslovakia, an important link in the German line of communications to the Russian front. Due to almost complete cloud coverage, the target was bombed by instruments and returning crewmen were unable to give any indication as to results, although indications were good that our bombs hit in the target area.

All of the aircraft, which, had taken off that morning, returned safely, Moderate flak was encountered along the route, but not one of our ships suffered so much as a scratch. As they had for so many missions, the Luftwaffe fighters stayed away from our formation, either remaining on the ground, or being off somewhere else in the blue.

The three hundredth mission was completed just a few days short of 20 months after the first mission. On March 31, 1943 the original air echelon of the Group bombed Villacidro Airdrome, in what was then Nazi held Sardinia, taking off from the first of our two African bases. Since that day our Forts have ranged the skies over the entire Mediterranean and central European area, dealing destruction to enemy installations in many countries. Bombs of every type have been dropped on airdromes, marshalling yards, factories, oil refineries, harbors, bridges, submarine pens and ordnance depots. Not content with devastating these strategic targets, our aircraft have given vital aid to the Ground Forces whenever called upon for tactical support. Every invasion, from Sicily to southern France, was precluded by the work of our Fortresses, and the hard pressed Allied soldiers at Anzio, Cassino, and other points of fierce German defense were heartened and helped by the close support given them by our planes.

One of the first heavy bombardment groups in the Mediterranean Theater, the 99th has always been in the forefront of 15th Air Force activities. When the Wing of B-17s was chosen to fly the historic, first shuttle-bombing mission to Russia, the 99th was picked for the lead group, and it was a ship piloted by our present Group Commander, Colonel Lauer, which set the pace. Ploesti and Vienna, the two places which have felt the greatest weight of the 15th Air Force bombs, know well the power of the 99th.

Statistics tell the whole story of our activity and the records are many and imposing. Behind all these figures lies a human story — a story of men. Courage, devotion to duty, the will to win and hard work are those hard to measure qualities which made the 99th a great organization. Three hundred missions was not the goal, nor will four hundred be. The goal was defeat of the enemy and a return to a better world.

LIFE WITH THE 99th AT HOME AND ABROAD

On the first day of June, 1942, at Orlando, Florida, part of the equipment was located for a group which still had no personnel. The orders for the activation of the 99th Bombardment Group (H) were cut and later the equipment was transferred to Mac Dill Field, Florida to Barkdale, Louisiana and then to Pendelton, Oregon.

It was on the 25th of September, 1942 that orders were cut at Gowen Field, Boise, Idaho, activating the personnel from the

29th Bombardment Group of the 2nd Air Force to form about a 20 percent strength of the new group from the 6th, 43rd, 52nd and 411 Squadrons. These squadrons formed the nucleus of the 246th, 347th, 348th and 416th Squadrons in that order.

Colonel Fay R. Upthegrove was designated as the Group Commander, and Lt. Colonel Leroy Rainey as Deputy Group Commander.

Departing from Gowen Field on the 26th of September for Walla Walla, Washington, the advance detail and part of the equipment arrived and the real work of the Group began with the arrival of the rest of the cadre by the end of the month. Additional ground personnel arrived from the Salt Lake City Army Air Base Replacement Center in Utah.

In the month of October, the Group received 12 flight leaders and their crews. Flying one plane per squadron, with the Squadron Commander and a model crew flying each, the minimum number was increased during the month to 10 aircraft for the Group.

On November 10th four Operations Officers were assigned to the Group from Goven Field.

So, because of the poor weather, the Group moved from Walla Walla, to Sioux City, Iowa to complete its second phase of training at the base where it was already scheduled to take third phase training. The movement took place in the middle of November. Adding more aircraft and crews, as well as acquiring about 75 percent of the ground crew's total strength, the Group, by the 18th of the month, really became a working organization.

The Group lost its first crew and aircraft during an accident in training on November 30th, when No. 286 crashed three miles from the field.

All the equipment was packed and ready to go between December 31, and January 4, and the ground echelon entrained midst a driving snowstorm of blizzard proportions for satellite fields at Mitchell and Watertown, South Dakota. The 348th, 416th, and Hq. Squadrons went to the former, and the 346th and 347th headed further north to the latter base.

Meanwhile, the air crews went to Salina, Kansas, arriving on the 5th of January, 1943, for the final stage of air training. From the 7th to the 13th, the combat crews were on leave while the ground crews "hup, two, three, four" and got in some sack time at the satellite bases with "no planes, no work, no nothing."

The flight echelon flew to De Ridder, Louisiana, after returning from the leaves. Despite some little engine trouble and what-not coming overseas, the trip via Morrison Field, Florida, Borinquen, Puerto Rico, Atkinson Field, Georgetown, Brit. Guiana, Belem, Brazil (where a couple of the 348th ships collided and were held up for repairs) to Yumcum Field, Bathurst, Gambia, and finally across the Atlantic Ocean to Marrakech, Morocco. Three of the Squadrons proceeded to Oran and the 347th followed later.

At the La Senia AAB, Algeria, the crews got final briefing and with the various lectures felt themselves ready for combat by March and two squadrons each proceeded to the 301st and 97th bases. After the work was completed on the Group's own field at Navarin, (not far from Constantine) the crews and aircraft moved in.

Meanwhile, the ground crews still in South Dakota until the latter part of February sweated out the rumored furloughs and, after much ado, received a six day "furlough" without traveling time to be taken either at the time of changing stations from South Dakota, to Tinker Field AAB, Oklahoma City, Oklahoma, or from the latter base upon arrival.

In March the Group's ground men were considered "processed" and proceeded to Camp Kilmer, New Brunswick, New Jersey, arriving March 19, 1943.

Measles seemed to be the order of the days at Kilmer and some of the barracks were continually quarantined with that disease, hikes, drill, lectures, guard duty, obstacle courses, calisthenics, and games, K.P. etc. etc., were supplemented by passes to New York and nearby cities and town. Finally, all was in readiness and after many restricted periods, the ground men packed up and entrained for Weekhawken, New Jersey on the morning of the 28th of April, 1943. Detraining there, the Group was ferried to Staten Island where the men and equipment were bundled and crammed aboard the U.S.S Edmund B. Alexander, staying overnight in the docks and pulling out early in the morning, the 29th of April, 1943, (about 19 1/2 months ago) and the ground echelon began to draw its overseas pay.

Limping across the Atlantic Ocean with faulty engines, the Alexander and its very precious cargo dropped far behind the rest of the convoy and were escorted by two Navy destroyers which provided ample protection from the lurking U boats. A safe landing was made at Oran, Algeria, at 1930 hours May 12, 1943, and the men were moved to a bivouac area at La Senia.

At the La Senia base, ground men were visited by members of the air echelon and learned about the operations out of Navarin. On May 24th, the two echelons joined forces again after a long separation. The reunion was made possible only after a never-to-be-forgotten 40 and 8 ride in the super modern, deluxe, streamlined luxury jobs that the French run on their North African tracks.

The ground crews also learned about the first 21 missions from members of the air echelon and a small part of the dope is this. The first mission of the 99th was flown to Villacidro, A/D, in Sardinia, on March 31, 1943, with Colonel Upthegrove leading and the largest number of B-17's to be used in the war to that date, 94 was employed with the 99th and two other groups sallying forth. The men had loaded the bombs, kept up the ships, flew'em and started all over again in the cycle until the rumored coming of the ground men became a reality. Great celebrations took place as friends got together again and the 99th was once more intact so the war wouldn't, it couldn't, last long.

The 25th mission was flown on the last day of May, when our Group bombed the Foggia A/D in Italy for the longest mission to date, and the bombs destroyed many enemy aircraft grounded on the field.

Missions, excursions, and the war, all continued during the month of June. Reports of an expected Arab uprising had all the men carrying arms at all times for a few days, but it proved to be a dry run and was soon forgotten.

On the 36th mission to Messina, Sicily, on June 25th, the roughest opposition in flak and fighters to that date was encountered and though the target was well covered, the enemy had taken its toll of the 99th men with two killed and eight wounded.

The next day was a rough one also, although it was a non-operational day, as an explosion of 500 pound bombs which occurred as they were being unloaded from trucks, caused the death of 16 men and critical injuries to four more. The men were all from the Ordinance company and the Service Squadron men who were driving the trucks.

Colonel Rainey left the Group on the 29th of June and Colonel Richard Smith took over the post of Deputy Group Commander. Another old timer in the Group, Major Frank Dunnington, S-2 Officer was also transferred out on this date.

Dust storms and heavy concentration of dust particles on every object in the area proved to be one of the greatest nuisances of the period. Fireworks on the Fourth of July were limited to another explosion at the Ordnance dump and a large fire in the wheat fields nearby. Luckily, this time there were no casualties although a great deal of hard work was necessary to quench the fire.

More fireworks and great disaster occurred on the 5th of July as the 99th attacked airfields at Gerbini, Sicily. Led by Colonel Upthegrove, this mission Number 41, was successful in the amount of damage done to the enemy target, but it also was heavy in casualty losses to our own Group as one complete element was shot down. Later on several of the men on the crews returned and reported on the whereabouts of others hitherto unreported. Staff Sergeant Benjamin F. Warmer, III, was credited with shooting down seven enemy aircraft from his waist gun position in a 348th ship. The Group later received a Presidential Citation for this mission.

On the night of July 9th a special invasion mission was pulled to Sicily and the invasion was made early in the morning with one more step taken toward the end of the war. Missions to Sicilian targets came thick and fast about this time and on the 14th of July the Group flew its 50th mission to Messina, Sicily.

The first Allied attack on Rome, on July 19, mission No. 54 was flown with the 99th dropping 108 tons of 500 pounders on the marshalling yards and railroad buildings in the area. Great care was taken by the crews which had been briefed not to drop any stray bombs in the area of Vatican City and other non-military targets and the mission was highly successful. Two movie photographers and three internationally known newsmen made the flight with the 99th. The newsmen were Raymond Clapper of the Scripps-Howard papers, later killed in a crash over the Marshall Islands in February 1944, Richard Tegaskis in the International News Service and Herbert Matthews of the New York Times.

Foggia marshalling yards were the targets for our 56th mission on July 22, and the Group encountered severe opposition and lost a crew and a plane as well as receiving damage to several other aircraft.

Another move was in the wind in the last week of July 1943, and as we prepared to move to Tunisia, reports came through that Mussolini had resigned as leader of the Italians and we had high hopes of a quick victory.

By August 6th our new quarters were well under way and the field at Oudna, near Mohammedia, a few miles from Tunis was ours.

From Oudna, our first mission was in Messina, Sicily, and was Number 61, and we hit the target well. We brought back three wounded men though we didn't escape unscathed.

The big event of August 14th was the Bob Hope show at the 301st B. G. field across the way and many our venturous souls went over the hills to see his troupe (of course France's Langford might have drawn a few of the wolves — could be).

The 99th's first mission to France took place on the 17th of August when the LeTube A/D at Marseilles, was smashed and many enemy aircraft were caught on the ground with their "flaps down". Other damage was done that day to hangars, and ack-ack batteries.

Axis mentors decided to give us a taste of bitter medicine and almost got close enough to us to give us a scare as their aircraft attacked Bizerte, lighting up the skies and the ground crews were made to realize a little that there actually was a war going on.

Foggia again was a target for the 99th on the 25th of August on Number 66 as we destroyed 41 enemy aircraft on the ground and 28 others were hit by the Fortresses. We lost one crew of the 416th, however, and one man in the 348th was killed and three others wounded, all because of flak from enemy guns.

Lt. Gen. Spaatz, and Maj. Gen. Doolittle were present at the 99th field to present the Distinguished Service Cross to Staff Sergeant Benjamin Warmer, III for his record in bagging seven enemy aircraft on the July 5th mission.

The 348th lost a crew and ship over Bologna on September 2nd. The seventh of the month will be remembered by the same squadron for it lost a bombardier on that attack.

The same day Commanding Officer of the Squadron, Major Warren Whitmore, and his crew were on their 50th mission as was the veteran aircraft Number 494. While over the target, Major Whitmore's ship was hit badly and he couldn't land it at the base, so as the ground crews sweated out the slowly dropping crew members "chuting" to earth one by one, the Major kept circling the field in 494 and then bailed out himself with the ship crashing a few miles away. All 11 men on the crew were ok with minor injuries received on landing.

The day of the 72nd mission (to the Frascati A/D near Rome) proved to be an historical one in the course of the war, for Italy was at the same time invaded and the country capitulated on paper.

Mission Number 88 was the 99th's first mission to Germany and a ME factory near Augsberg was to have been the recipient of the bombs but an undercast caused the Group to turn back. Lt. Franck, a 416th Bombardier, was credited with 4 enemy aircraft, and Staff Sergeant Warmer got credit for the 10th of his career. We lost two crews and A/C and others were wounded and damaged.

Greece was first hit by our bombers on the 9th of October as Salonika and Larissa had targets for our bomb loads.

There was little operational activity from the 11th to the 23rd of the month when ground members took transports for bases in Italy and Sicily and the remaining ones began to wonder what was in the wind. The crews with two days rations and supplies followed the ground men. The mission to Wiener Neustadt was a washout and the planes and men returned on the 25th. The men told marvelous tales of the improved conditions in Italy compared with our dust hole in Africa.

Mission Number 100 proved to be an operational flop, as far as bombing goes, due to a complete overcast over Turin, but credit was given for the mission and the century mark was reached on the 30th of October 1943.

General Spaatz and Doolittle were present for our celebration of the 100th Mission and though rain hampered the festivities, it didn't stop the barbecue and beer party

Another overnight deal was on for the 2nd of November and with Sicily as the refueling spot, and Wiener Neustadt again as the target, the detail was SNAFUED.

On the 11th, the Group reached the latter target and did a good job on the aircraft factory there. En route we destroyed eight enemy fighters and lost none.

We had a man wounded and one killed from the 346th Squadron on the 16th of November, and on the 18th, Staff Sergeant Streetman, and aerial photographer of the 348th (originally of the 416th), saved a ship and crew by freeing a lodged frag bomb that would most certainly have destroyed both ship and crew. With about 30 seconds to go before explosion time, he pried the bomb loose with a machine gun barrel and sent it earthward.

On the 19th, the B-25's of the 310th Bomb Group left our field and some Wellingtons or "Wimps" of the RAF dropped in on us.

On the 25th of November came Thanksgiving Day, and it proved to be the biggest and best eating day we had overseas.

We also said goodbye to Colonel Upthegrove as he left our Group for the USA on DS and Lt. Colonel Thurman took over the reins as Acting Commanding Officer.

Plans were made during the last week for a move to Italy. Pay day brought gold seal greenbacks as the medium of exchange and the francs of North Africa were converted to a reasonably accurate facsimile of our US cash.

The first contingent of men left for Bizerte on the third of December.

Mission Number 112 to Grissano was flown and both ships and crews stayed overnight at our new base in Italy It was the sight of many wrecked enemy aircraft, and at the time, the base was occupied by South African units.

The big guns could be heard when the rest of the 99th arrived at the new base, for the front lines weren't so many miles away, and the nights were at first a little ominous. Trips to the Marshalling yards and vicinity were taken and it afforded the crews an opportunity to see at close range what damage they had wrought upon at least one of their erstwhile targets. Air raid dry runs became frequent and as the field really began to take shape and tents were erected, and offices set up, the 99th again prepared to operate from a permanent base. The first mission pulled from the new A/D was made on December 14 to Athens, Greece.

On December 15th Colonel Charles W. Lawrence succeeded Colonel Upthegrove as our Commanding Officer with Lieutenant Colonel Thurman as his deputy.

The same day the crews had a rough mission to Augsberg, Germany which cost the lives of two men, wounds to four, and 20 were listed as MIA, as well as the loss of two of our aircraft. Jerry paid in the loss of at least eight fighters.

On Christmas Day of 1943, the Christmas parcels to the Axis from the 99th Bomb Group were to have been a nice load of bombs delivered via air, but since the weather prevented the crews from seeing the targets, the presents were returned to the base for future delivery. A super-duper Christmas dinner was cooked for all hands and a large shipment of mail and packages came into boost the morale of the men no end. Another happy occurrence on Christmas Day was the return of one of the crews that was lost on the 19th.

All sweated out the explosions on the 29th as a landing "Wimpy" crashed into a parked one and fires and explosions followed thick and fast.

Another turkey dinner with fixin's topped off the first day of the New Year and everyone wondered just what 1944 would offer.

January found many improvements in living quarters, if not in weather, although a fine month was made operationally with 24 missions completed.

On the 19th and 20th of the month the Group participated in a softening up attack on Airdromes in and around Rome and our targets for the day were respectively Ciampiano and Contocelle.

These attacks were not without reason, however, and on the 22nd of January the Allies landed south of Rome and the invasion was number one topic on discussion.

On the 26th of January Lieutenant Colonel Thurman again took over command of the Group when Colonel Lawrence became commander of the 5th Wing

January 27th proved a bad day for the 99th as a Wellington crashed in the Squadron area hurting several men and killing the First Sergeant of that unit, Sergeant Peter Hurey, (later the enlisted men's mess hall was named Hurey Hall in his honor and memory). For their work in the dangerous surroundings during the accident, eight men received soldier's medals.

February ushered in a new month and a new contingent of WAC's to town. Few of the men were in a position to make any time with them, however, as the lads stationed in town took over pretty quickly. Not much doing operationally but there were some good movies during the month to brighten up the recreational side of the picture.

On February 15th Colonel Ford J. Lauer assumed command of the Group, relieving Lieutenant Colonel Thurman.

February 25th provided us with a fine target for the day, Regensburg, Germany, Number 156, and the target was destroyed with the loss of four aircraft. We had destroyed 21, probably 22, damaged one of the aircraft in the severe running battle with 150 Nazi planes that occurred that day.

March found a lot of work being done on the A/C as the insignia of the yellow diamond which had earned us the title of "Diamondbacks" was outlawed and we had this replaced with a "Y" insignia.

On the 15th Cassiono was attacked, a stronghold for the Germans, and our mission number 161 was highly successful.

We were not too happy at the exchange deal that sent our nice new G's to the 2nd Bomb Group in exchange for some pretty well beat up - F's and rumors flew thick and fast as to the whys and the wherefores of the exchange.

Members of the 483rd Bomb in the 416th Squadron area hurting Group arrived with new aircraft (G's) and were attached to us for a time awaiting the arrival of their ground crews. Later on we got their G's and they got the F's that we had. Our first mission in the silver jobs was to Steyr, Austria.

Easter Sunday church services found nearly everyone in attendance at one time or another during the day. A nice, lazy non-op day was observed on this Sunday holiday.

On the 16th of April, Lieutenant Colonel Headrick, our Deputy Commander, was lost in a raid over Belgrade, Yugoslavia, as the Group met intense flak.

Cokes put in an appearance on the 17th and the one per man was very welcome after nearly a year sans coke.

On April 23rd our Group, led by Colonel Lauer, went to an aircraft factory at Wiener Neustadt, Austria, and tossed lethal "monkey wrenches" into the works, hampering production of Herr Hitler's Luftwaffe replacements. Encountering no little opposition from Nazi ack-ack and fighters, the Group received another Presidential Citation later on for this mission.

During April, we also got order on insignia and a "Y" on a diamond background became our designation and mark of recognition.

The Group almost completely destroyed the Varcse A/C factory on the 30th of April on Mission No. 184 and we suffered the loss of two A/C and crews and had six wounded men on the aircraft that returned.

May 12th provided a day for another two missions, as one was pulled in the morning to the Tarquinia A/D north of Rome, and in the afternoon, the target most vital at the time was headquarters of the German High Command in the same area, and the surroundings received a heavy pounding from our missiles.

Toward the latter part of the month many rumors were spread about another "something big cooking". The rumors became fact as on the morning of June 2nd a mission got under way and the crews with new uniforms, complete with all insignia, and stripes, identification, etc., bombed the Debreczen M/Y in Hungary, and continued on to a base at Poltava, Russia. While the men rested, worked, and spread international good will among the Russians, those left behind sweated them out, got sack time, swimming, etc., and waited for their return. They pulled a mission from Russia and returned to the Stalin base. Coming back to our base on the 11th the crews told tales of Russian hospitality, of wine, women and song, entertainment, sightseeing trips, and in case we forgot to mention it, they told about the women of Russia.

July was another theatrically big month as Irving Berlin and his "This Is The Army", show played in the Foggia area for a few days. It was also a good month operationally as we flew 21 missions.

On the 14th of July, Colonel T. J. Meyer assumed command of the Group relieving Colonel Lauer who went home on DS. Colonel Meyer became ill and after his transfer to the hospital,

Lieutenant Colonel James A. Barnett became the Commanding Officer, taking over on the 1st of August.

On August 12, 13, and 14, the Group bombed gun installations on the northern Mediterranean Coast and it began to look as though something big was in the offering and it was. On the night of August 14th a pre-midnight briefing revealed the invasion of southern France early the next morning. For the first time in the history our heavy bombers took off in darkness and arrived at the beachhead just before the first waves of invasion troops swarmed ashore.

August gave us a total of 22 missions and several men returned to the base after enforced vacations in POW camps in Rumania. They were released when that country capitulated to the Allies.

Hitler's Navy received a bad blow on the 4th of September as we bombed Genoa Harbor and sub pens and destroyed at least four of the subs therein.

Major General Nathan Twining, Commanding General of the 15th AAF, was on the field on the 27th of September to present the Group with the streamer of the Presidential Citation for its work on the Gerbini Airdrome on July 5, 1943. He commanded not only the men who flew the mission but also those on the ground whose work made it possible.

On September 22, Colonel Lauer returned from the States and once again assumed command of the Group relieving Lieutenant Colonel Barnett.

Also in the month of September our Executive Officer, Lieutenant Colonel William Hampwn, a member of the Group since "way back when" departed for the USA, as did Lieutenant Colonel Lawrence Semans, our Operation Officer. Their places were filled by Major John A. Sarosy, former Group Adjutant, and Lieutenant Colonel Bernice S. Barr. Captain N. M. Scarborough came up from the 347th Squadron to become adjutant.

October found the 99th with a total of 16 missions flown with a couple of days being, "double days", with "Red" and "Blue" forces going for different targets. The seventh provided targets in Vienna, Austria and Nove Zamky, Hungary respectively. On the 13th Blechhammer South O/R, Germany, and the Florisdorf O/R at Vienna were attacked, in the drive to cut off Hitler's oil production and keep his machines inactive.

On the 12th of October, anniversary of the day when Italy's Chris Columbus is reputed to have discovered America, the Group flew Mission No. 275 and in direct support of the ground troops, dropped a part of the heaviest bomb tonnage ever to be released in a tactical operation.

A day and night combination of a double mission day also took place when on the 23th of October, the Klagenfurt, Austria, aircraft factory and the marshalling yards at Munich were hit.

In November, we were again visited by Major General Twining, who presented the second streamer to the unit's colors as recognition by the President of work done on April 23, 1944, at Wiener Neustadt, Austria. He also presented Captain Warren Christianson, of the 347th with a DSC at the ceremonies.

Our Group's 300th Mission occurred on the 20th of November, as targets at Bruno, Czechoslovakia were hit. Thus, we start upon another leg of a journey toward the end of the war and start another page in the Group history.

GROUP'S ACTIVITY IS SHOWN BY STATISTICS

Captain Philip Sweeney of the Group 5-3 Section, Statistical Officer, has unearthed some figures and facts for our amazement and edification.

In the 300 Missions, we have had 8,746 aircraft take off on missions and of these 8,111 have gone over the target, leaving the remarkably low number of early returns at 635. Thus, each mission we have averaged sending out 29 aircraft and averaging only two early returns, with 27 dropping their bombs on enemy objectives.

These 8,111 aircraft over the target have dropped 18,938.14 tons of bombs on enemy targets, or an average of 63.29 tons per mission. The B-17's most popular bombs were the 500 pounders as 51,915 RDX and General purpose bombs of that weight were carried, weighing 1,270.74 tons. Also the 1,000 pounders numbering 4,748 and tipping the scales at 2,374 tons were unpleasant gifts to the enemy. Five thousand seventy-seven 100 pound Gp's weighing 253.85 tons were dropped; six thousand seven hundred and sixty-eight bombs of the 250 pound class for a total of 846 tons; 5,572, 300 pounders totaling 835.8 tons; 292 bombs weighing a ton each, busted blocks in many a district in Nazi held territory. More or less as an experiment, 28-1,600 pound anti-personnel bombs were dropped weight, 22.4 tons. Conflagrations were started by our 552 bombs of the 100 pound incendiary variety, weighing 27.8 tons, and by our 348,500 pound fire makers at 87 tons.

Gunners have fired 2,269,343 rounds of ammunition in combat at 1,954 enemy aircraft and have destroyed 459 of them, probably destroyed 96 more and damaged 59 of the 1,954. Thus 614, or 31 1/2 percent of all these aircraft encountered were at least hit. All of these were met prior to Mission Number 210. The aircraft also destroyed 556 enemy aircraft on the ground and only ten of those since Mission Number 200.

So far, the enemy hasn't done too well against us (knock on wood if you wish) as in 300 missions they have damaged 1,372 of our A/C by flak, and enemy aircraft succeeded in hitting 162 of ours. Enemy action has accounted for the loss of 60 of our aircraft and nine others have been destroyed by other causes, mostly of an operational nature, since coming overseas.

Personnel who have flown with us, and some who are still flying with us under the colors of the 99th total 3,359 men. Nearly one-half of this number 1,460 have completed 50 missions, and 1,030 are still flying with us.

Major Frederick Koehne, Group Flight Surgeon, has also furnished us with a few pertinent facts and figures as to personnel in combat.

Of the total of 81,110 man sorties, only 892 have men with misfortunes including 88 men killed in action, 251 wounded in action, 216 missing in action, 97 in Prisoner of War Camps and 3 interned in Switzerland. 147 more fortunate men have returned to the base after being either MIA or POW's.

AIR CHIEFS PRAISE GROUP ACHIEVEMENT

The Group received messages of congratulation from the following Air Force leaders:

Major General Nathan F. Twining, Commanding General of the 15th AAF:

"To the 99th Bombardment Group at the time of their completion of 300 Missions. I extend my most sincere congratulations. Despite the diverse handicaps that confronted the 99th during the early days of the war, the shortage of planes, the lack of spare parts and the many other adverse conditions the Group continued to strike the Hun. The 15th Air Force is proud of the magnificent record and accomplishments of the 99th."

Brigadier General Charles W. Lawrence, Commanding General of the 5th Bombardment Wing:

"It is indeed a pleasure to add my congratulations to the 99th Bombardment Group upon completion of 300 combat missions against the enemy, especially since I had the honor of commanding the Group during part of its combat service.

"The 99th Bomb Group has sustained an enviable reputation of dependability and achievement. The ground echelon having establish a record in the care and maintenance of equipment second to none in the Air Force; the combat personnel a record of sustained operations of superior caliber throughout its entire service in the Mediterranean Theater of Operations.

"The Wing is proud of you. Continued success and happy landings!" Brigadier General Charles S. Born, A-3, 15th Air Force:

"My most sincere congratulations to the 99th Bombardment Group on the completion of 300 Missions.

As one of the senior heavy bombardment groups in the Army Air Forces today, and as a very senior outfit in the European war, you are to be highly commended for the outstanding record of your group."

Brigadier General Fay R. Upthegrove, Commanding General, 304th Bombardment Wing:

"Sincere congratulations to the Ninety-Ninth on the successful completion of Three Hundred Missions in the Theater."

"Starting from scratch a little over two years ago, when the Group first began to form, you have, indeed, come a long way. As to your record, it speaks for itself, there is none finer anywhere."

"It will always be the highlight of my life that I was fortunate enough to be your first commander; to organize, train, move overseas, and lead the Group through its first hundred missions. Having flown most of my combat missions with the Group, it will ever hold first place in my affection. Bound up in this affection are the hardships, uncertainties, adventures, and associations we shared. I owe a great debt to the Group that I can never repay."

"The sturdy, faithful planes, the fighting spirit of the combat crews, the tireless work of our ground crews, and our group staff and administration personnel have made the 99th the proud Bomber Unit we are today."

TWO ORIGINAL FORTS STILL WITH GROUP

Adorned with painted bombs, swastikas, and patched flak holes, they stand proudly in their revetments, veterans of many combat missions, the B-17 F's now used as transport ships with the 99th. Stripped of their arms but not of their dignity, these aircraft, original ships of the original crews made the Atlantic crossing in February, 1943.

Two of these majestic bearers of ill tidings to the Axis are still with us and performing perhaps a little less glorious task than their younger "sister soldiers of the skies," the G's, but still serving ever-loyally the Group which has cared for them.

The Warrior, or as the records carry her, A/C number 29474, is assigned to the 347tn Squadron, and witl Master Sergeant Walter K Boothe, crew chief, nursing her through her ills, flew 96 combat missions. Out of 102 attempts, only six times did she turn back from the goal.

Aircraft number 49472, or Sweater Girl, a 416th ship got her name from the voluptuous replica of femininity which adorns her frame. This lady of the airlines flew 111 missions in combat, a mark made possible by careful handling by the crews in the air and by the ground crew chief by Master Sergeant Chester A. Smiechowski.

Another one of these "Queens of the Air" is no longer with us, but one well worthy of mention. Number 29513, with 121 missions to her, bears the name "El Diablo". At present flying General Upthegrove hither and yon, at a B-24 Wing in this theater, "El Diablo" earned the respect of our former commanding officer who requested her transfer to him. General Upthegrove well knows what "The Devil" can do - he should, he ferried her across the Atlantic himself nearly two years ago.

They have served us well in combat, are serving us as transports and may they continue to serve as they have done, veterans among veterans.

A SALUTE TO THREE BUILDERS OF THE 99th

In addition to the various Commanding Officers, who have been responsible for the success of the 99th, three other officers, who are no longer with us, have had major roles in the growth and development of the Group since its activation. They are Lieutenant Colonel William H. Hampton, Lieutenant Colonel Lawrence S. Semans, and Lieutenant Colonel Vernon E. Fairbanks.

Colonel Hampton, as Group Executive Officer, was the administrative bulwark of the Group, working tirelessly to see the unit functioned without friction and red tape. He relieved the Group Commanders of all the little problems which crop up from day to day, and he deserves credit for the smooth way in which the Group functioned on the ground. Colonel Hampton left the Group in September, on orders taking him back to the States, where an important assignment awaited him.

Colonel Semans began his long tour of duty with the Group as Commanding Officer of the 347th Squadron, taking that unit through phase training, and leading it overseas. Shortly after landing in Africa he was transferred to Group, and given the highly important position of Group Operations Officer. Under his able supervision, schedules, training programs, combat tactics and SOP's were established which did much to make the Group a tight and effective combat unit. Colonel Semans put great stress on safe and intelligent flying, cutting down on Snafus and helping to make the 99th's record lowest on losses, both combat and non-combat. He, too, let us in September for a well deserved furlough in the States.

Lieutenant Colonel Fairbanks, (Doug to one and all), came overseas as acting Group S-2, but the acting part was soon dropped, and he became head man in the Intelligence Section. A veteran newspaperman, he could divorce fiction from fact, and when he briefed the combat crews, in the "hour before dawn," they knew they could stake their lives on his information. Colonel Fairbanks' light could not long be hidden under the Group's bushel, and back in April, he was called to Wing to head its A-2 Section.

SPECIAL SERVICES ALWAYS ON BALL

During 19 months overseas there was much to be proud of and much to be laughed off and forgotten in the way of Special Services activities. To be forgotten are the days when at Navarin the Special Service Officer had to call the Photo Section to find out if the Group would have "Pierre of the Plains" that week - or no movie at all. A man's social life consisted of an occasional gin rummy game by candlelight and vino; sports activities usually got no further than competing with flies for the daily ration; and in the way of education, a person was doing well if he had learned to say "combine" when the occasion presented itself.

By the time we got to Italy troubles had straightened out somewhat, as attested by the completion of the great serial "Arsenic and Old Lace". In the way of athletics, the only activity going on in the Wing area was basketball and the 99th out shone all other groups by going through the season undefeated. They became Wing Champs after defeating the 82nd Fighter Group, and went on to copy the Area Crown by toppling the 12th Air Force contender the 21st Engineers. Co-managed by Captain Scarborough, 347th and Captain Kirkendall, 346th the team did much to bring the name of the 99th before the Air Force sports eyes.

COFFEE, DOUGHNUTS, SMILES ON TAP IN "BEA'S CORNER"

A combat mission may not be all beer and skittles, but the end of it finds coffee and doughnuts waiting for the returning flyers. After they have stowed away their gear, piled on the trucks, and have been driven up to answer the probing questions of the eager interrogators, the tired crewmen break for "Bea's Corner," where they get the best coffee in Italy, and a fistful of crisp, sugary sinkers.

"Bea," or Margaret Risdale as she is formally known but never called, is in charge of all Red Cross Cubmobile units servicing the Wing area, but her heart and her person are always with the 99th. Through the heat and the dust of Africa to the heat and the dust and the mud and the cold of Italy, she has sweated out ETA's, waiting for her boys to come back. Overseas as long as any of us, she looks as sweet and fresh as the day she left the States. Bea hails from Philadelphia, which is to the everlasting credit of that fair city, but to all of us she is the kind of American girl we left behind in the cities, towns and hamlets of home.

Anyone can hand out coffee and doughnuts, but the smile Bea hands them out with makes all the difference in the world. As each man passes her counter, and exchanges a few words with her, he feels she has been waiting just for him. It's hard enough for a girl to turn on a stock smile for several thousand men over a period of many months, but when she can make that smile warm and sincere, she's tops. That's Bea, the "Sweetheart of the 99th".

On the few occasions when other girls have substituted for her, the men have never failed to ask, "Where's Bea?" No slight is intended to the other girls who are all wonderful - it's merely the most sincere tribute we can pay to our best friend. Thanks for everything Bea!

FIVE WINNERS OF DSC TOP LIST OF 99th HEROES

In a unit which has been in combat over a long period of time, many men will have performed acts of heroism, exhibited superb skill, and shown a devotion to duty, which has inspired those around them. The 99th has had more than its share of heroes, and the Group is proud of its long list of award winners.

Heading the list are five men who exhibited extra-ordinary heroism while participating in aerial flight against the enemy. To these men has gone the second highest honor awarded by our country, the Distinguished Service Cross. One man gave his life in winning the medal, and the award was made posthumously. He was Lt. Thomas C. Hawke, a bombardier with the 347th Squadron.

On a mission to San Giovanni, Italy in July, 1943, Lt. Hawke was setting his sight on the bomb run when a piece of flak hit him in the throat. Despite the intense pain, shock and loss of blood, Lt. Hawke stayed with his bomb sight and successfully dropped his bombs on the target. He would not accept aid until his work had been accomplished. He died shortly after reaching a hospital.

Lt. John W. Wiley, 347th Squadron, was awarded the DSC for the encourage he exhibited on a mission he flew as a co-pilot. Under attack by enemy fighters, his plane was badly hit by cannon fire, and Lt. Wiley was knocked out of his seat and one arm was severely wounded and rendered useless. Unable to help with the controls, Lt. Wiley still managed to be a useful crew member. Dragging himself along the bottom of the cockpit, he kept feeding ammunition to the top turret gunner until the enemy planes had been driven off. Hospitalized for many months, Lt. Wiley returned to combat and finished his tour of duty.

In the historic attack against Gerbini Airdrome in Sicily, which earned for the Group a Presidential Citation, one man stood out above all the others. The hero of the day was Staff Sergeant Benjamin F. Warmer, a waist gunner with the 348th Squadron. When the big, blonde, sharpshooter had finished his day's work, seven Nazi fighter planes had been shot out of the skies by his cool trigger efforts.

Another gunner, Staff Sergeant Slavomir Nepil, of the 346th Squadron, was the next man to win the coveted award. In July, 1944 he flew a mission to Ploesti, in his usual position, tail gunner. Nearing the target the ship was attacked by enemy fighters, after it had been forced to drop out of formation due to engine trouble. Sgt. Nepil's arm was shattered by an explosive shell, and succeeding shells, ripping into his compartment, threw him about violently. Despite this, and the intense pain he was suffering, Sgt. Nepil continued to operate his guns with one arm, until they were destroyed. Retiring from his position, he saw other members of his crew bailing out, and he was just able to leave the ship and pull the rip cord before losing consciousness.

Most recent winner of the DSC was Captain Warren C. Christianson, a lieutenant with the 347th Squadron when he performed the act for which he was later decorated. In August of this year, Captain Christianson was piloting an element lead ship on a mission to Vienna. On the bomb run his ship was hit by flak, but he managed to keep his element in formation, and a successful pattern of bombs was dropped. Over the target, Captain Christianson's plane was hit again by flak, and an entire engine was torn from its mounting. The B-17 was thrown into a spin, but Captain Christianson, disregarding his own personal safety remained at the controls, allowing all the other members of the crew to abandon the ship. After dropping many thousand feet, he finally succeeded in pulling the ship out of the spin at a very low altitude. Without the aid of navigational charts, or crew members, Captain Christianson flew the plane all the way back to the base, where he made a safe landing despite one useless tire, loss of an engine, and damaged controls.

In addition to the five men named above many others have merited awards, and to date members of the Groups have earned 8 Legion of Merit Medals, 29 Silver Stars, 209, Distinguished Flying Crosses, 45 Soldiers Medals, 26 Bronze Stars, 245 Purple Hearts, over 2,500 Air Medals, and innumerable clusters to the latter.

15th AAF IN ITALY

Taking a break after the ceremonies during which the 99th Bombardment Group received The Distinguished Unit Citation at the 15th AAF Flying Fortress Field in Italy are

(Left to Right) **Brig. Gen. Charles W. Lawrence, Orlando, Fl., Brig. Gen. Fay R. Upthegrove, Olean, NY., Col. Ford J. Lauer, Kansas City, MO., (C.O. of the 99th BG), Mrs. "Bea" Ritchie, Red Cross Worker, and Maj. Gen. Nathan F. Twinning, Commanding General of the 15th Army Air Force.**

CHAPTER 14

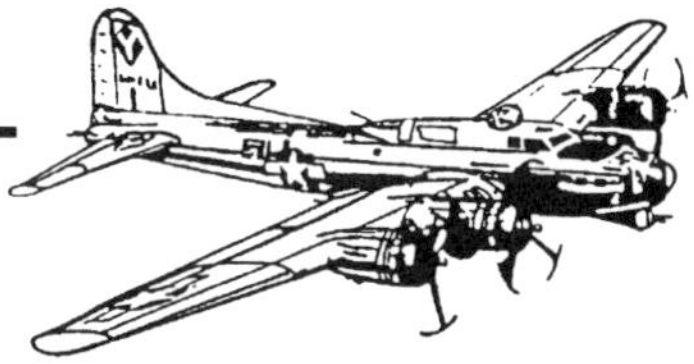

The Glamour Of War

After my 50th Combat Mission on October 31, 1943, I was still wearing my gold bars of Second Lieutenant. The crew was happy for me as I was now ready to join others back in the States and new assignments. Captain Burrell, now Major Burrell, had a talk with me as to what I would like to do when I returned to the United States. I frankly told him that I wanted out of B-17's and would like to become an instructor in Basic or Advanced training back home.

Bankhead and I were talking about my return one afternoon when Major Scarborough opened the tent flap and said, "Is this what you are looking for?" He threw a half sheet of paper on the wooden floor and left. I did not move so Bankhead got up and read it. "Jim," he said, "you have been promoted to First Lieutenant." Bankhead then told me I could have his silver bars he saved after his Captaincy came through. He pinned them on me. I was happy because they were proudly worn by him for over a year. I learned later at Miami Beach that the orders of promotion had been given by official radio on 20 October, 1943 and copies of the order were not available.

I was going home and my family and friends were looking forward to my coming home.

A letter from General Arnold, the Commanding General of the Army Air Forces, read in part:

"It is desired that you make every effort to instill in the minds of military personnel being returned to the United States the necessity for impressing upon our trainees some of the glamour of war and the great personal satisfaction to be derived from actually hitting the enemy between the eyes. Explanation should be made of the boost in morale and enthusiasm which will result from proper discussion of their experiences in actual combat.

To you, officers and enlisted men who have been through actual combat, it is entrusted the serious problem of training new units. One of the most important duties you will have is to build the morale of the personnel under you up to a point where they will be anxious to maintain the high standards you have set in this theater."

Though I had little contact with Major Burrell during my last few missions, he did ask me to co-pilot for him on a flight to break in a new engine of a B-17. "Jim," he told me, "it's like old times." The old times were over one year ago when I was his hand-picked co-pilot for combat and my wife and I sat beside him as he played the piano for the dances back home. You can imagine my surprise when Harry wrote up my Recommendation for my return to the United States. I got the transfer I requested and some of the kindest words a commander could give his men. I have always treasured the following letter from Harry:

CONFIDENTIAL
(Equals British CONFIDENTIAL)

THREE HUNDRED FORTY SEVENTH BOMBARDMENT SQUADRON
NINETY NINTH BOMBARDMENT GROUP (H) ARMY AIR FORCES
Office of the Squadron Commander
APO 520 NATOUSA

2 November 1943.

SUBJECT: Placement of Experienced Combat Crew Personnel Returning to the United States.

TO : Commanding Officer, 99th Bombardment Group (H), AAF, NATOUSA, APO 520.

1. This is to certify that 1st Lt JAMES F. BRUNO, 0-729804, a member of this organization since 30 October 1942, has been relieved from Combat Flying Duty as a Pilot upon completion of fifty (50) Operational Missions in accordance with policy set forth within this Theater.

2. This officer has demonstrated worthiness of promotion, but due to existing Table of Organization and authorized grades, this officer along with others in his status have been held in grade without fault, bad character, or misconduct on his part.

3. This officer is highly qualified to fill a duty greater than he has filled within this Unit due to his combat experience and standards of an Air Corps Squadron. Highly recommend 1st Lt James F. Bruno, 0-729804, for transfer to single or twin-engined aircraft.

HARRY R. BURRELL,
Major, Air Corps,
Commanding.

201 - Bruno, James F. (0) 1st Ind. FRU/heg

HEADQUARTERS, 99TH BOMBARDMENT GROUP (H), AAF, NATOUSA, APO 520, 2 NOV 1943

TO: Whom it may concern.

1. Approved.

2. Request the recommendations of the Squadron Commander be followed in the placement of this officer.

3. The undersigned certified that subject officer has completed 50 combat missions and 312:40 operational hours.

RAY R. UPTHEGROVE,
Colonel, Air Corps,
Commanding.

1 Incl: Certificate of
Group Flight Surgeon.

CONFIDENTIAL
(Equals British CONFIDENTIAL)

On my return to the States I was given a ten day leave after which I and all others returned to the redistribution center at Miami Beach. There, after several weeks, the men were assigned to their next station. We were examined by a doctor who wanted to find out what went on in our heads. He was unable to figure me out and kept me almost a month longer. He even wanted to meet my wife and I at the dance in the hotel. I danced with his little redhead and he danced with Irene. I was getting desperate to go to my next station and asked him to send me out as my dear wife was about to bankrupt me with her shopping at the exclusive Lincoln Road Dress Shops. I was also losing the flight pay of $90.00 per month.

The orders finally came through and I was sent to Central Instructors Training School at Randolph Field, Texas. It was the "West Point" of the air at that time. I was given only one ride of less than four hours to qualify for flight pay. The First Lieutenant told me I gave him a "very good" ride and was impressed by the way I handled the twin-engine Beechcraft.

After the month was up, I called to headquarters and told my orders were to proceed to Ellington Field near Houston where I was assigned to be an instructor. I took the orders and proceeded with my wife to Houston.

I drew a wonderful Captain as my Squadron Commander, G. D. Cowan, who was one of the best instructors and had earned a "Green Card" at Bryan, Texas. He showed me how they were taught to bring the plane down through the clouds with ceilings below some 500 feet. Even though I passed my test for a White Card," I never felt safe on instruments.

I was soon given a class of students to teach the advanced flying technique to and the "Glory of War." My students were a group of talented college graduates and I had no trouble getting them to graduate. To my surprise, none of them wanted to go to Four-Engine Training. They selected B-25's or A-26's for combat. However, the Army had the last say. My best student, whom I recommended to go to four-engine, was left at Ellington to fly navigation training in the Lockheed Lodestar. So much for recommendations.

After graduating the first class of students, I was made Squadron Commander for the next class. I enjoyed the position and at the time of graduation the evaluation team from Randolph, Texas rated my squadron the only "Superior" one out of the eight. I did not know there was any competition going on among the training squadrons.

CHAPTER 15

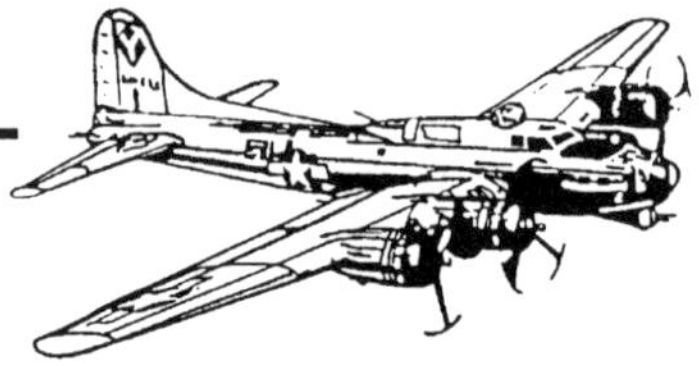

The F.B.I. Questions My Loyalty

In May of 1944, I received a phone call from the squadron to report to headquarters. Upon arriving there, I was told two men were in a private office who wanted to speak to me. The two men introduced themselves as agents of the F.B.I. They showed me their credentials. They had been looking for me for over a year, I was told. This was a surprise to me.

Their first question to me was, "Do you know a Dr. Bruns?" "Why yes, I beamed. "He is a good friend of mine." They quickly looked at each other. The frank answer caught them by surprise. Margaret Truman had written in her book, "Murder at the CIA" the F.B.I.'s most guarded secret was, "Don't Embarrass The Bureau." I had done just that with my first answer.

Had I denied knowing Dr. Bruns, the agents had my own letter to the doctor, written in October 1942 from Gowen Field, Boise, Idaho. They read it in part to me. These were the words that put them on my trail:

"Doc, this B-17 is a wonderful airplane. It takes off with 42 inches of mercury"

They wanted to know why I wrote that to him. I told them I was acting smart as the planes he was flying at Waukesha County airport did not have that instrument. My explanation was accepted. They did ask if I knew the doctor was a Nazi sympathizer.? I told them that before we were ready to go overseas from our base in Des Moines, Iowa, we received a ten day leave to go to our home. My wife was with me and we drove my 1939 Chevrolet home. My wife was not to return. One person I most wanted to visit was Dr. Bruns. I wanted him to see my silver wings and my new bride, Irene. We did have a cordial visit. As my wife and I were going out the office door the doctor came up to us and said, "Jimmy, we are making a big mistake, the Germans are a great people." It set my wife and I back a little, but we had already said goodbye and had shaken hands. As we left the building, my wife and I discussed his remark and shook it off as a natural thing for a German to say. My wife's parents were of German decent. I told the agents about the meeting with the doctor and how my wife and I did not attach much to it. Again, they were satisfied with my frank remarks.

I told them my civilian instructors had stated to the pilots I had little chance of surviving the rigid Air Corps pilot training. The doctor came forward to defend me and told me I would make it. He will make "a good Army pilot" he stated, in the presence of my other friends and my two instructors. This explanation was the key to my continuous correspondence.

Since they wanted to know more about Dr. Bruns, I suggested they go to Randolph, Texas and talk to a Major George Light. Dr. Light was at the head of the School of Aviation Medicine and was also a Civil Aeronautics flight examiner. He shared an office with Dr. Bruns prior to Pearl Harbor. This brought a sudden halt to their questions.

Their next statement was, "This investigation will never hurt you. Don't ever mention it to anyone, not even your wife."

The abrupt ending of our meeting precluded any further conversation.

In retrospect, I was not expecting, nor was I prepared for the F.B.I. investigation. I did not understand the meaning of their parting statements, "This investigation will never hurt you." I was not even to mention it to my wife! Was my being cleared a blessing in disguise?

Frankly, I felt like the "Prisoner of Chillon" as Lord Byron had portrayed him:

At last came men to set me free
I ask'd not why, and reck'd not where.
So much a long communion tends
To make you what you are,
It was at length the same to me,
I'd learned to love despair.
Even I regained my freedom with a sigh.

The two agents never explained why the F.B.I. had waited eighteen months after I wrote to Dr. Bruns about the B-17 to contact me. Two questions revealed they had not done their homework. The question, "Where were you, we have been looking for you for a year?" I was in North Africa, flying B-17s, was my answer. Another question - "Why did you stop writing to Dr. Bruns?" For nine months, since August, 1943, there had been no more letters for them to read. "The doctor was asking questions I felt he should not be asking, so I stopped writing to him in August," was my answer. I was in the States on transition training prior to going overseas for over five months. The letter about the B-17 was sent to the doctor in October, 1942. I went overseas in February, 1943.

What went on after the meeting and what the Agents revealed to the Base Commander at Ellington Field was never known to me. My officers file, the 201, must have had many good reports on my character and my flying. The suspicion by the F.B.I. was removed. I do believe an apology was made by the agents on behalf of the Bureau.

By the end of the week I was offered an assignment any pilot would love to have. It was a transfer to Wright Field, Dayton, Ohio. Wright Field was the home of the Materiel Command. Had I gone there, I would have worked with Captain Robert S. McNamara to revolutionize the Air Force Procurement System. I would have been one of the "Whiz Kids." After the war, the Ford Motor Company hired the entire crew.

Having told the officer to give someone else the chance, they came back in a few days. This offer was to take over a squadron commander's position. This I accepted.

I loved the job and got along well with my instructors. In my first meeting with them I stated I would accept nothing but their best performance. When they gave me a cadet they assumed was not doing well, I gave a check ride. I would find where the instructor had failed on teaching a certain procedure properly. Every student passed.

Little did I know the eight squadrons were in competition. Nor did I know the Standardization Board was on the base to grade the work of each squadron. At the end of the Advanced training for the class, our squadron won the only "Superior" rating. I was promoted to Captain. The promotion caught up with me at Fort Worth, Texas. I was sent there for B-24 training.

After being in limbo until my return from North Africa and the F.B.I. investigation in May, 1944, I had duplicated Captain Burrell's positions within one year. As an advanced flying instructor for one class, I was the squadron commander for the next class. Then, after a B-24 course, I became a Four-Engine instructor. In a few months, I returned to Ellington field and was promoted to the Operations Officer of the Pilot and Navigation Training School.

For many years the investigation by the F.B.I. played on my mind. I was not happy in the manner they had conducted it. Every day, I repeated the names of the two agents, wanting to mention them in the book I intended to write. The day I wrote the Bureau, April 24, 1970, the two names were erased from my memory. I was upset with my being sworn to SECRECY about their meeting with me. I was hoping the reply would reveal their names. It did not. J. Edgar Hoover replied to my letter himself. I was given permission "to accurately describe my contact with the representatives of the Bureau".

J.Edgar Hoover's letter follows.

OFFICE OF THE DIRECTOR

UNITED STATES DEPARTMENT OF JUSTICE

FEDERAL BUREAU OF INVESTIGATION

WASHINGTON, D.C. 20535

April 30, 1970

Mr. James F. Bruno
1460 Carriage Lane
New Berlin, Wisconsin 53151

Dear Mr. Bruno:

In reply to your letter which I received on April 27th, I have no objection to your accurately describing your contact with representatives of this Bureau. Our interview of you in April, 1944, was in connection with an official inquiry dealing with our responsibilities in the internal security field and did not involve any investigation of you personally.

Sincerely yours,

J. Edgar Hoover

THE INSTRUCTOR — THE UNSUNG HEROES

Long before Pearl Harbor, the Army Air Corps had no conflict which called the pilots away from American shores. They routinely trained the pilots who qualified for duty. The planes were out-moded, the P-36 being one of them.

I remember one of our hometown pilots, a Second Lieutenant by the name of Melcher, who came to the Waukesha County airport with a P-36 in 1940. It was awesome to see him fire a cartridge to start its engine and belch smoke as it roared to life. After a short warm-up he taxied out for a take-off; the assembled crowd was thrilled! It was then I decided I would love the glamour of the military life of flying than be a commercial pilot.

The following year, Lt. Melcher returned to the airport, this time sporting First Lieutenant bars and flying a silver AT-6 trainer. He made two low-level passes at less than 50 feet across the field with the roar of the 850 H.P engine splitting the eardrum. Everyone, including myself, was fascinated with the high pitch sound as he made the parting fly-by.

I was more determined than ever to enter the ranks of military flying after Lt. Melcher' s second visit.

When I graduated from twin engine advanced as a cadet on September 29, 1942 I became a co-pilot in the right seat of a B17-F and on my way to combat. By a stroke of good luck, my squadron commander and first pilot was Captain Harry R. Burrell. Harry was an instructor in twin engine and four engine aircraft prior to Pearl Harbor. He was also the check pilot for our bomb group training for overseas deployment.

The morning Captain Burrell was to check me out in the left seat as the first pilot, he gave me the bad news. Combat crews were formed the night before. We would no longer become first pilots. We were going overseas. Being the squadron commander of the 347th squadron, he told me I was to be his co-pilot. He had selected a top navigator as well as a top bombardier. Apparently, he was able to evaluate them by their school records.

After Harry had to give up his crew, being moved to group operations, he gave me an equally fine pilot. First Lieutenant H. Blaine Bankhead had also been an advanced flying instructor before Pearl Harbor. He could handle the B-17 like he was flying the single engine planes he had instructed in. That base was Maxwell Field in Alabama.

In my days at Ellington Field in Texas, I was to meet another great instructor. Major Richard Bong also in service prior to Pearl Harbor was given instructor duty. He, at first, hated that assignment. After the war in one of his few interviews, he did admit the hours he spent as an instructor served him well in his air battles with the Japanese pilots. His 40 confirmed kills were proof. He spent a few minutes counting and recounting my air medal and oak leaf clusters. I was embarrassed. The Distinguished Flying Cross I earned on 25 May, 1943 would have made me feel better. As he shook his head, I knew he wanted to ask about some other medal I should be wearing. He was about to speak, then decided not to. As I was preparing to answer, I, too, changed my mind. We nodded "Good Bye" to each other. Two weeks later, I was unusually saddened as I read about his fatal crash in the F-80 Shooting Star. Until then, I had looked ahead to a future day when I could visit him in his hometown; Poplar, Wisconsin.

My own days as an advanced instructor at Ellington and as a B-24 instructor at Forth Worth, Texas were rewarding. Because of the urgency to get fighters and bombers to the theaters of war, we graduates were not able to spend a year as instructors after graduation. From my observation, the pilots who had over a year or two in the Air Corps were the finest men you wanted to be a part of your team. You could say they were "seasoned pilots."

After instructing my first class of cadets, I was promoted to be one of the eight squadron commanders. It was a chance to further evaluate your instructors and their students. Not all instructors fall into the same pattern. When they gave me a student for a check ride or washout, I found many times the student was not as inadequate as he was made out to be.

My evaluation and report to my instructors of "E" flight of July 27, 1944 was outlined for them.

SECTION "B"—2517 AAF BASE UNIT, ELLINGTON FIELD, TEXAS

OFFICE OF THE SQUADRON COMMANDER
GROUP III, SQUADRON "E"

27 JULY 44

SUBJECT: Progress Check Rides

TO: All Students & Instructors:

1. Recent checks have shown that students errors were as follows:
   - (a) Gliding air speeds not constant. (Glide 90 M.P.H. on landings, power off)
   - (b) Students are retracting wheels before 25 feet of altitude is attained.
   - (c) Students are doing stalls very improperly. All students read and be familiar with throttle, prop and cowl flap positions for power on and power off stalls.
   - (d) Students throttle technique in taxiing very poor. Using too much throttle, making turns too fast and spinning around on one wheel. Both wheels should be turning at all times.

(e) Students are not sounding off on GUMP and Single Engine Drill. This must be done.

JAMES F. BRUNO
1st. Lt., Air Corps,
Squadron Commander

When the class was ready for graduation, I was happy to hear we had won the only "Superior" rating by the Central Flying Training Command. The headquarters were at Randolph Field, Texas. It resulted in a promotion to Captain.

CHAPTER 16

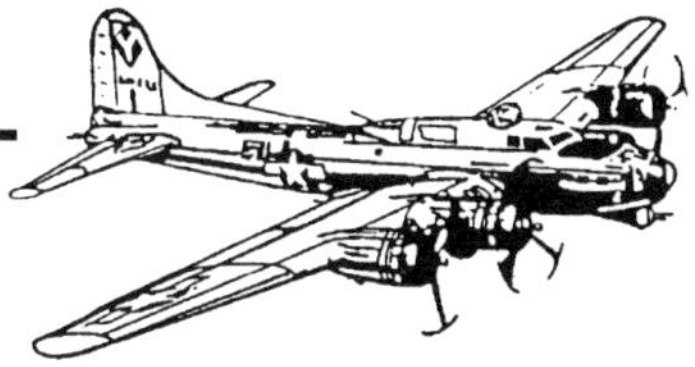

FORT WORTH AND B-29 TRAINING

Saying good-bye to Mrs. Dub Harbeson and leaving the lovely ranch home was not easy to do. We spent the most pleasant six months of my Army Air Force career at Houston. We were not looking forward to making new friends and finding other housing. After my last tour in four-engine, I certainly did not look too kindly on the new orders. However, we packed and drove to Fort Worth following another couple, Major Eddie Broussard and his wife.

Eddie had been Director of Personnel at Ellington since his return from combat duty. He had worked his way up from the ranks as an enlisted man and gone to Cadet Training from Houston and won his wings in true Story Book fashion. He was the enlisted man's idol.

Upon reporting to Tarrant Field in Fort Worth, we found a group of fourteen men had been selected from various bases throughout the training command. All held good positions which they, too, did not want to leave for a second tour of combat.

The training in B-24 Liberators got underway with most of the former B-17 pilots finding the flying characteristics much different. The tricycle landing gear, however, was much easier for landing. I was always cutting the power back on the downwind leg as we did on the B-17 and found the B-24 did not have any of the gliding characteristics of the B-17. I was forced to apply considerable power to keep from undershooting the runway.

The relationship between instructor and student had been rather good for the first two weeks, although we did resent the instructors telling us, "This is the way it is done in combat." They had never been there and we wished they had been stressing how to handle the flying of the plane and the necessary emergency procedures.

After the second week at Fort Worth I was summoned to report to the office of the Director of Training. The Lieutenant Colonel returned my salute and said, "Captain, do you always park in someone else's parking space? I replied, "No, Sir." Again he repeated the question. "Captain, do you always park in someone else's parking space?" When he began to grin, I suddenly realized he had addressed me as "Captain." He reached out to shake my hand as he handed me my promotion orders. This was an unexpected surprise and I had no idea why I should receive a promotion while a student in B-24 training.

That night at the B.O.Q. I showed the promotion orders to Major Broussard. He was elated and asked me if I had gone to purchase a set of Captain bars. That was completely out of my mind that day, and I would have waited for the weekend before spending the $2.00. I was wearing Bankhead's First Lieutenant bars he gave to me in North Africa less than eleven months earlier and hated to remove them. Eddie insisted we go to his room where he had his set of bars saved since his promotion to Major. He wanted me to go to class the next morning wearing the new bars. After all, the Squadron Commander of the instructors was a Captain and by date of rank all fourteen students out ranked him.

Since Eddie was in the personnel office back at Ellington, I asked him why I was promoted? "Didn't you know, he told me, your squadron received the only "Superior" rating by the Training Command Evaluation Board?" How was I to know? We had left for Fort Worth immediately after the Board had completed their inspection. I realized then it was the hard work of the men under me, both officers and enlisted men, especially the 1st Sergeant, that contributed to the promotion.

The next morning, my instructor was green with envy when he saw the Captain bars. He changed from that day on and before the week was out, I had been assigned to a Second Lieutenant. The former instructor was a much better teacher than his replacement. The new Second Lieutenant would gather his students together at 8:00 A.M. and hustle them out to the plane to be the first one off the ground. The other instructors were amazed no one else could beat him at getting off first. I had him pegged from the start. Rather than explain the day's lesson to the four students at the blackboard, as the other instructors were doing, this Second Lieutenant would dash out to the assigned plane with his students and shout the day's lesson over the roar of the engines to each student.

The following week, a Colonel Schweitzer flew in from Washington in a B-25.

Several days later, the Colonel received a report on our progress and called us into a group meeting. "You men are the nucleus of a new B-29 Heavy Bomber group," he said. "You will be the Squadron Commanders and Flight Leaders; you will be promoted in rank."

After the group meeting, we each received a separate interview behind closed doors. Here we could all frankly discuss our thoughts relative to the mission proposed for us.

From the treatment I had received from my instructors during the past three weeks, I was in no mood to go to the Pacific Theater. I informed the Colonel I had just received my Captain's bars and intended to wear them awhile. I stated I would instruct in B-24's and in B-29's until the day I saw these instructors on their way back from overseas, with ribbons on their chests; only then would I be ready to go over again.

The Colonel's mission failed to materialize as only one man out of the fourteen was ready to go back. We had seen too many men who had spent years as instructors and never got out of the United States. We continued the training as it was determined to let us complete the transition course.

One day we had an actual emergency procedure that I completed before he was aware we had one. The propeller governor on number four engine failed and the propeller wound up out of control. I recognized the unusual whine immediately and hit the feathering button. Nothing happened! I retarded the throttle of the over-speeding engine, cut off the fuel supply, closed the cowl flaps and cut the ignition switch. I also advanced the power to the other three engines and closed the partially open bomb bay doors to reduce drag - this procedure took less than 15 seconds. Lieutenant Finch suddenly became aware of the overspeeding prop and asked if the emergency procedure should be undertaken. The two students standing behind watching me told the instructor I had already completed it.

We then took a course for a landing back at the home base. The instructor called the tower and requested them to prepare us for an emergency landing. We were some five miles out when we were cleared for a straight landing on runway 18. We had been about 75 miles north of the field when the emergency occurred. The instructor was noticeably concerned over the prop spinning out of control and nervously watched it, hoping it would not come slicing into the cockpit. He made no attempt to take over or ask to land the plane. This was fine with me, so I brought the plane down easily with the three good engines.

After the end of our training we all had to read and initial the report of our progress by the instructors. Lieutenant Finch had written up my airborne emergency. He stated, "the student reacted very calmly without fear or excitement." Little did he know this had happened to me in combat on the Messina mission with a squadron of enemy planes diving at us for good measure. There was nothing to fear this time and no gunners to direct and caution to conserve ammunition.

RETURN TO ELLINGTON

After a few months of instructing in the B-24, the group of fourteen combat veterans were again reassigned to bases throughout the State of Texas. I was the lucky one, returning to Ellington where I was welcomed by the pilots and friends I had made there.

Major Eddie Broussard was sent to bombardier school in West Texas. After pulling a few strings, he was reassigned to Ellington so he could be back in his favorite City of Houston.

The mission at Ellington had changed considerably when I returned. There were fewer advanced training squadrons and the emphasis shifted to that of an advanced navigation training school. The pilots were checked out in C-47 type aircraft and Lockheed Lodestars. The Lodestars were modified to carry six to eight navigators on training missions. I was happy to find one of my former students, 2nd Lieutenant James Griffith, had been retained as a pilot for the navigation training school.

I was given the job of Operations Officer of the Navigation School. I was to understudy Captain Charles Steen and his assistant, who was also a Captain, and in due time they would be transferred to a combat unit for eventual overseas duty.

Another officer, whom I will refer to as Major Sid, had just recently reported to the base. He and I were checked out in both of the navigation aircraft and received our instrument ratings in them. Major Sid was assigned to the Maintenance and Engineering Section. He was a B-24 combat veteran and one of the pilots who participated in the daring low-level raid on the Ploesti Oil Fields in Romania. Sid became a good friend during our transition training.

An A-26 was assigned to the base during our stay at Ellington and caused much comment among the pilots. Everyone wanted to fly it, as all had heard what a good low-level attack bomber it had proved to be in combat. To eliminate the number of pilots flying it, one of the Deputy Commanders had restricted its use to Majors and above. This irked a great number of pilots, especially the newly graduated Second Lieutenants. These men were eager to get checked out in anything that was "hot!" and this A-26 surely was one of them.

The first time I was involved in "buzzing" was during an official flight to Randolph Field from Ellington. I had taken a Second Lieutenant along with me in an AT-6 and had estimated one hour and eleven minutes as the flight time to Randolph. I turned over the controls to the Lieutenant while over the open spaces. He signaled to me from the front seat with a "thumbs down signal" and I nodded my head in approval, as I thought he wanted to check something. He put the plane in a steep dive and pulled out twenty feet off the ground. He stayed at tree-top level for a considerable distance. I continued to think of what we could do if the engine began acting up? The thought went through my mind the only way out would be to pull the stick back, pull up to at least 1,000 feet, roll the plane on its back and bail out.

How does one explain such a foolish act? From several thousand feet of altitude a pilot could belly a plane into a pasture and at least have a valid story along with a plane which was still repairable.

Many times there happened to be a pine tree ahead off the right wing or the left that was higher than twenty feet. The Lieutenant never pulled up over it - he would merely raise the wing enough to miss the tree and set it back down after passing it. He was a real professional at "buzzing," which led me to believe many cadets had indulged in the practice, though it was "strictly forbidden!"

We finally arrived at the outskirts of Randolph and had to climb to get into the traffic pattern. On our return trip, I made sure we stayed above the 500 foot minimum flight level required by Civil Air Regulations for flight over unpopulated terrain.

The job of Operations Officer was not an easy one. The administrative paper work and constant decision making for flights was enough to make you wish you had returned to combat. Also, a pilot who is bound to desk work gets "rusty" on his flying, navigation and instrument work. Without an assistant, after the two Captains departed, I was working long hours and the fatigue was much worse than I experienced in combat.

One afternoon, while sitting at my desk wondering why I had accepted such a trying job, a Major Adams walked into the office and said, "Captain, I got you this job." I managed to respond with a very weak "Thank you!" I had planned to give up the Operations position in favor of flying navigators. I wanted to build up hours to help me obtain an airline job some day. Major Adams informed me "You can have this job as long as you want it. Your orders from now on will come out of Washington and no one else can tell you what to do."

I thanked the Major.

He was leaving the next morning, and told me he would return in a few months. That was November, 1944. He returned in January. Wanting to get into the regular Army, I asked if he would check the list in Washington to find out if I had been recommended for a regular Army commission.

Military began the build-up after Pearl Harbor and all volunteers and inductees were designated being in the AUS, (Army of the United States). We were to serve for the duration of the war, plus six months. After that time, we were civilians again.

When the Major returned in March, 1945, I was informed my name had not been placed on the officers to enter the regular Army. That gave me the option of getting out or we could choose staying in the service and reverting to Second Lieutenant or to an enlisted status.

I was still without an assistant, although the school operations were coming along in fine shape. I was not getting needed rest. With over two hundred pilots and some three hundred navigators, I felt responsible for their safety. Sometimes I would cancel a mission, being concerned weather would be a hazard to flying. I did not want pilots flying instruments on night missions if a storm was in the forecast. To have planes making landings at scattered air bases due to weather was not to my liking.

The war in Europe was going well for our Allies with Hitler and his armies being decimated. Told that my position called for promotion to Major gave me nothing to be happy about. The promotions were frozen due to the Allied forces about to end the fighting in Europe.

Still the Major was interested in my well being. On his return to Washington, he told me he was slated for a special mission to London and would see me upon his return.

In May, 1945 a special meeting was held at the theater. An announcement was made that men who had accumulated 75 points or more would be eligible for discharge. My decorations and overseas time came to 225 points. Irene and I discussed the discharge form. We decided an airline job would be much better than the stress I was under.

About a week later, I was given the assistant I waited a year for. The officer was a Major. I was told to teach him the operations work, and together, we would run the base. That meant the Major would command the base, calling for the promotion to full Colonel. I would soon be the deputy base commander that called for Lt. Colonel. I was enjoying my work at last. We each spent a half day at the job, and the other half in flying or other activity to our liking.

Oblivious that I had applied for the discharge, I was sitting on top of the world.

I was being checked out in a twin engine Beech, used for official flights, when the tower called me to land. My discharge had come through. With heavy heart, I cleared the base, ready to be a civilian again!

The Major told me he was planning on selling his home in Kansas City and purchase a liquor store in Houston. Such an announcement surprised me. The military must not have been to his liking. Each of us left behind the carefree flying that was ours. The B-25 was the plane I missed the most. We had a P-40, however, I decided I wanted no part of it. The AT-6 we flew in advanced was always a great plane to punch holes into the clouds.

Before I completed clearing the base, an order came from the Headquarters, Army Air Corps, stating all operations officers were to report to Bryan, Texas, the instrument training school.

Those pilots graduated with a "Green Card." It was the coveted card. "Green Card" pilots were few. They learned to become so proficient they could land a plane when weather conditions would ground the average pilot with a "White

Card." Most pilots with "White Cards" passed the instrument test in simulated conditions. While passing the tests in various aircraft, including the B-24, C-47, Beech-At-7 and Lockheed Lodestars, I never felt comfortable filing an instrument clearance.

I learned later, upon applying for an airline position, the first question asked was, "Do you have a "Green Card?" When I replied, "No," the interview was over. The application, however, was given to me and for over 50 years it has yellowed in my desk.

My discharge became official at Fort Sheridan, Illinois on September 13, 1945. I had an accident with my 1941 Pontiac one month later. To the police officer called to the accident scene, I said, "I told the Sergeant at Fort Sheridan not to discharge me on the 13th!"

CHAPTER 17

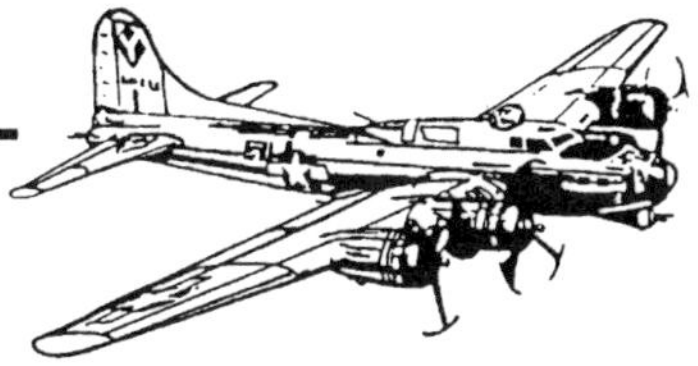

A Few Heroes

MAJOR GENERAL FAY R. UPTHEGROVE

During my training and 60 missions I had very little contact with General Upthegrove. When I obtained his address from Harry Burrell's mother in 1968, 1 began writing to the General and told him I was going to write a book on the 99th.

In my four year correspondence with General Upthegrove, (1970 to 1974), I was able to learn how and why all of his officers and enlisted men loved and respected him. He graduated from West Point in the Class of 1927.

The General sent me photos, commendations, awards, press releases and personal letters from his men and many other stories and events untold to anyone. He shared with me about his family and their careers. He mentioned the death of his first wife and the loneliness it brought to him. In his Christmas, 1974 letter and card, he informed me that by a quirk of fate he met a high school and early West Point sweetheart, Betty Staley Sackett, whom he had not seen since 1946 when his mother died. She had no children and she had lost both her mother and husband in 1973. He wrote, "The old attraction still existed and grew on visits in May and June, so they decided to share their remaining years and were married on October 1, 1974." As happened with many children of the Army Air Corps men, they were to visit their sons or sons-in-law in the new Air Force.

Among the many articles sent me during the 1970's by General Upthegrove is this poignant story of man's love for man.

Our bomb group did not participate in the Ploesti oil field raid. Captain Eddie Janic and my classmate, George Black, were there. Major Sid Zelinski, whom I served with at Ellington Field, Houston, Texas, was also there. He spoke very little about the raid. It was fellow pilots who told me he was on the raid in B-24's.

'GREATER LOVE HATH NO MAN THAN—'

MAAF HEADQUARTERS, Feb. 20—The Congressional Medal of Honor has been awarded posthumously to Lt. David R. Kingsley, of Portland, Ore., a 15th AAF Flying Fortress bombardier who gave his parachute harness to an enlisted gunner and went down with the crippled ship.

The first Medal of Honor to be awarded a member of the 15th AAF was for heroism on a mission by the 97th Bomb Group to the Ploesti oil fields on June 23. The incident was not made known until survivors returned months later from a Bulgarian prison camp.

During an attack by enemy fighters, S-Sgt. Michael J. Sullivan, of Chicago, a tail gunner, was injured and his parachute harness ripped. Other gunners carried him to the radio compartment where Lt. Kingsley administered first aid.

Damaged by fire from both anti-aircraft and enemy fighters, the Fortress was seized by terrific vibrations and the pilot gave orders to bail out.

"After everyone had cleared the ship," Sullivan said later, Lt. Kingsley picked up my parachute harness and discovered that it had been ripped by cannon fire. He did not hesitate a moment, but took his own off and adjusted it on me."

"Carrying me in his arms, Lt. Kingsley struggled to get me through the door into the bomb bay. He told me to be sure and pull the rip cord after I had cleared the ship."

"I did, and as I was floating down I saw the plane fall off and go into a spin. It crashed, exploded and burned. The last I saw of Lt. Kingsley, he was standing on the catwalk over the open bomb bay doors.

"Bulgarian soldiers later showed us a charred billfold with a picture of Lt. Kingsley and cards belonging to him. They said they had taken them from a body in the wreckage."

** COMMENDATIONS **

Major General Upthegrove was given high praise for the accuracy of the bombing by the 99th Bomb Group he headed. Two Presidential Unit Citations were given.

Maj. General F.R. Upthegrove
First Commander of the
99th Bomb Group

HEADQUARTERS FIFTH WING (US)
APO 520

11 June 1943.

SUBJECT: Commendation.

TO: Commanding Officer, 99th Bomb Group, APO 520.

1. The following is a message received from General DOOLITTLE:

"SPAATZ MESSAGE TO DOOLITTLE PARAPHRASED AND FORWARDED FOR YOUR INFORMATION I WISH TO COMMEND COLONEL UPTHEGROVE AND HIS GROUP ON THE EXCELLENT BOMBING OF THE IMPORTANT REFINERY AT LEGHORN THE BOMBING WAS ONE OF SUCH ACCURACY AS TO DESTROY COMPLETELY A MAJOR PART OF THE INSTALLATION AND TO RENDER THE ENTIRE PLANT INOPERATIVE PD CONFIRMED BY PHOTO RECONNAISSANCE THE RESULTS OF THIS ATTACK ARE AMONG THE BEST YET ATTAINED IN THIS THEATRE"

2. This is another of the many commendations received by units of this command. It is hardly necessary that I add to this my comments, however all units of the Fifth Wing (US) have made such notable achievements in this theater of operations that I cannot help being justly proud to have such units under my command.

J.H. ATKINSON,
Brigadier General, U.S.A.,
Commanding.

HEADQUARTERS FIFTH WING (US)
APO 520

8 July 1943.

SUBJECT: Commendation.

TO: Commanding Officer, 99th Bomb Group, APO 520.

1. The following message was received at this Headquarters and is forwarded for your information.

THE FOLLOWING MESSAGE FROM SPAATZ IS QUOTED FOR YOUR INFORMATION QUOTE ACM TEDDER EXTENDS APPRECIATION TO THE STRATEGIC AIR FORCE TO WHICH I ADD MINE FOR THEIR SPLENDID AND EFFECTIVE OPERATIONS YESTERDAY JULY FIVE PD THE PERFORMANCE OF NINE NINE HEAVY BOMBER GROUP DESERVES PARTICULAR MENTION CMA FOR THE SKILL WITH WHICH THEY CARRIED OUT THEIR MISSION AGAINST GREATER PART OF ENEMY FIGHTER OPPOSITION AND VERY HEAVY DAMAGE THEY INFLICTED TO ENEMY AIR FORCES IN AIR AND ON GROUND.

By Command of Brigadier General ATKINSON:

M.L. SECHREST,
Captain, Air Corps,
Adjutant.

1st Ind.
Hq. 99th Bomb Gp (H) AAF, APO 520, NATOUSA, 9 July 1943.

TO: CO's All Squadrons this Group.
1. For your information.
By order of Colonel UPTHEGROVE:

RUSSELL T. JACOBS,
2nd Lt., Air Corps,
Ass't Operations Officer.

LYS Z V LDNQ NRS

TO NOTARY

FROM LDNQ 140931 B

TO CO 99TH BOMB GROUP

GR—BT

EXAMINATION OF PHOTOS OF ALL GROUP ATTACKS YESTERDAY REVEAL THAT ONE BOMB WAS OUT OF TARGET AREA STOP NO DOUBT THIS BOMB WAS A WOBBLER BUT BOMBARDIER WHO DROPPED IT SHOULD BE JACKED UP A BIT JUST TO KEEP HIM IN LINE

ATKINSON

(Author's note)

This wire from General Atkinson was sent in a joking manner. Cannot find a date on it, therefore have no way of knowing which mission he mentions. General Upthegrove will be happy to see this one. This wire is better than a commendation.

ALLIED FORCE HEADQUARTERS
APO 512

19 August 1943

GENERAL ORDERS)

NUMBER 48)

1. I have received the following message to the Allied Forces:

FROM THE PRESIDENT OF THE UNITED STATES:

"All of us are thrilled over the Sicilian campaign now successfully concluded in accordance with the timing and planning of the Allies. This is especially true when we realize that the enemy forces in Sicily amounted to 405,000 men. The events of the past thirty-eight days show what can be done by team work based on preparation, training, timing, and above all on gallantry on land, on sea, and in the air. From the ancient Citadel of Quebec I send to you my warm congratulations, and to the officers and men under your command, British, Canadian, French and American, my thanks and enthusiastic approbation. Tell them 'well done.' Signed FRANKLIN D ROOSEVELT."

2. It is my desire that this message be brought to the attention of all personnel of this Command.

DWIGHT D. EISENHOWER
General, United States Army
Commander-in-Chief

DISTRIBUTION:
"D"

RESTRICTED
(EQUALS BRITISH CONFIDENTIAL)

ALLIED FORCE HEADQUARTERS
APO 512

20 August 1943

GENERAL ORDERS)

NUMBER 49)

1. I have received the following message from His Majesty, King George VI to the Allied Forces:

"On the final accomplishment of the occupation of SICILY, I wish to send to you and to all members of the forces that you command with such distinction my heartfelt congratulations on a great achievement. Throughout the BRITISH Empire, we have watched with admiration the ordered progress of the campaign by sea, by land and by air, and we rejoice at its successful conclusion. I should be grateful if you would convey to my BRITISH and CANADIAN Troops a special assurance of my pride in their share in this victory."

2. It is my desire that this message be brought to the attention of all personnel of this command. I am making immediate reply to His Majesty to express the intense gratification of the whole command in the receipt of this message and to assure him that the Allied Forces are ready to undertake any assignments our Governments indicate.

DWIGHT D. EISENHOWER
General, United States Army
Commander-in-Chief

DISTRIBUTION:
"D"

RESTRICTED
(EQUALS BRITISH CONFIDENTIAL)

RESTRICTED
(EQUALS BRITISH CONFIDENTIAL)

HEADQUARTERS
NORTHWEST AFRICAN AIR SERVICE COMMAND
APO 528

23rd August, 1943.

SUBJECT: Commendation

TO: All Units, Northwest African Air Service Command.

1. The following message has been received in this Headquarters from General Spaatz:

"From the President of the United States to the Allied Forces, the following message has been received: Quote All of us are thrilled over the Sicilian Campaign now successfully concluded in accordance with the timing and planning of the Allies. This is especially true when we realize that the enemy forces in Sicily amounted to four hundred thousand men. The events of the past 38 days show what can be done by team work based on preparation, training, timing, and above all of gallantry on land, on sea and in the air. From the ancient citadel of Quebec, I send you my warm congratulations and to the Officers and men under your Command, British, Canadian and American, my thanks and enthusiastic approbation. Tell them, well done, signed FRANKLIN D. ROOSEVELT Unquote. I desire this message to be brought to the personal attention of all personnel under your Command"

By Command of Brigadier General BARTRON:

/s/ David R. Stinson,
/t/ DAVID R. STINSON,
Colonel, G.S.C.,
Deputy Chief of Staff.

CONFIDENTIAL
(EQUALS BRITISH SECRET)

HEADQUARTERS G-29
NORTHWEST AFRICAN STRATEGIC AIR FORCE
APO 520 U S ARMY

27 August 1943.

SUBJECT: Commendation.

TO: Commanding General, 5th Wing,
Commanding General, 47th Wing,
Commanding General, 42nd Wing,
Air Officer Commanding, 205 Group,
Officer Commanding, 330 Wing,
Officer Commanding, 331 Wing.

1. The Commanding General is pleased to forward the following messages:

a. Message from Air Chief Marshall Tedder:

"My hearty congratulations to you, your commanders and crews, on success of their operations against the enemy air on 25 August. It is clear that success was obtained by care in planning and by courage and determination in execution."

b. Message from Lieutenant General Spaatz:

"I consider the Foggia attack of 25 August an outstanding demonstration of effectiveness of air operations well planned with intelligence and executed with spirit and ability. You, your staff, and the participating units are to be commended for a remarkably fine job."

2. In transmitting these commendations, the Commanding General desires to convey his appreciation for a task excellently accomplished.

By Command of Major General Doolittle:

S/ J.M. IVINS
Lt. Colonel, AGD
Asst. Adjutant General

CONFIDENTIAL

SECRET
(EQUALS BRITISH MOST SECRET)

HEADQUARTERS FIFTH WING (US)
APO 520

6 September 1943.

SUBJECT: Commendation.
TO: Commanding Officer, 97th Bombardment Group.
Commanding Officer, 301st Bombardment Group.
Commanding Officer, 99th Bombardment Group.
Commanding Officer, 2nd Bombardment Group.

1. The following teletype received at this Headquarters is forwarded for your information.

"THE ATTACKS CARRIED OUT BY UNITS OF YOUR WING ON BOLZANO CMA TRENTO CMA AND BOLOGNA WERE RPT WERE EXTREMELY EFFECTIVE AND MAY HAVE FAR REACHING RESULTS IN THE PRESENT SITUATION PD PLEASE CONVEY TO THE COMMANDERS OF THE UNITS CONCERNED MY CONGRATULATIONS ON THE SUPERIOR MANNER IN WHICH THEY ACCOMPLISHED THIS DIFFICULT MISSION PD GENERAL SPAATZ HAS ASKED ME TO PASS TO YOU HIS COMMENDATION ON THE EFFECTIVENESS OF THESE ATTACKS WHICH HE CONSIDERS OUTSTANDING PD"

By command of Brigadier General ATKINSON:

/s/ M. L. Sechrest
/t/ M. L. SECHREST,
Major, Air Corps,
Adjutant.

SECRET
(EQUALS BRITISH MOST SECRET)

ALLIED FORCE HEADQUARTERS
APO 512

7 October 1943.

GENERAL ORDERS)

NUMBER 58)

1. I have received the following letter to the Allied Forces:

"THE SECRETARY OF WAR"
WASHINGTON

September 24, 1943.

My dear General Eisenhower:

I wish to thank you personally and all the officers and men of the Allied Forces for your very kind wishes on the occasion of my birthday. The year just past in my life has seen the initiative pass definitely into our hands and has started us on the path to final victory. To you, your officers and your men goes a great share of the credit for the turning of the tide. Please extend to all ranks my congratulations and best wishes for their continued success in carrying the battle to the enemy.

Very sincerely yours,

(Signed) HENRY L. STIMSON

2. It is my desire that this letter be brought to the attention of all personnel of this command.

DWIGHT D. EISENHOWER
General, United States Army
Commander-in-Chief

DISTRIBUTION:
"D"

U.S. RESTRICTED
(EQUALS BRITISH RESTRICTED)

HEADQUARTERS
NORTH AFRICAN THEATER OF OPERATIONS
UNITED STATES ARMY

8 November 1943.

GENERAL ORDERS)
NUMBER 128)

MESSAGE FROM CHIEF OF STAFF, UNITED STATES ARMY

1. I have received the following message from General GEORGE C. MARSHALL, Chief of Staff, United States Army:

"I SEND TO YOU AND THE TROOPS UNDER YOUR COMMAND ON THE ANNIVERSARY OF THE INITIAL LANDING OF UNITED STATES TROOPS ON THE SHORES OF AFRICA THE CONGRATULATIONS OF THE OFFICERS OF THE WAR DEPARTMENT UPON THE GREAT ACHIEVEMENTS OF THE PAST YEAR. FROM THAT FIRST SLENDER FOOTHOLD, THEY HAVE MOVED FROM AFRICA TO SICILY AND ON TO ITALY, AND THEIR AIRMEN HAVE COVERED THE ENTIRE MEDITERRANEAN AND PENETRATED DEEP INTO THE EUROPEAN CONTINENT."

"TOGETHER WITH AN EXPRESSION OF PROFOUND ADMIRATION FOR YOUR ACCOMPLISHMENTS AND WITH CONFIDENCE IN THE VICTORY TO COME, I SEND MY PERSONAL CONGRATULATIONS AND THANKS TO YOU, THE OFFICERS, AND MEN OF OUR ARMY UNDER YOUR COMMAND."

2. I desire that this message be brought to the attention of all personnel of this command.

s/ Dwight D. Eisenhower
DWIGHT D. EISENHOWER,
General, U.S. Army,
Commanding.

LETTERS TO GENERAL UPTHEGROVE

22 December, 1944

Dear General Upthegrove:

I should have written much sooner than this, sir, but the wandering Burrell has been chasing around so damned much that he just hasn't written any letters. It doesn't take long to make up for a hell of a lot of lost time and the good old U.S.A. is certainly the place to do it. As you can see from the letterhead, I am still wandering around.

I flew back from Africa and made the states in record time – believe me, Miami really looked good. The Personnel Distribution Command have a wonderful setup in Florida and in two days I was on my way home for a 21 day leave (plus travel time) with everything from ration stamps to books on how the G.I. should act among the American natives. After a fine leave at home, I went to the Rehabilitation Center at Santa Ana, California for three weeks. Santa Ana is for bachelor officers and Santa Monica is for those entangled in marital ties. We received wonderful treatment there and except for physical exams, reclassification interviews and home front lectures, our time was our own.

Provisions were made for any type of recreation a person could want from golf to deep-sea fishing, but most of us spent our time and money in Hollywood. Flex was there and also Col. Shaeffer who took over the 347th when I left. Doc Newmans' brother is musical Director for 20th Century Fox and he really took care of us. This man power shortage certainly hasn't been overrated; females swarm like flies. Flex was operating true to form and when I left him, he was going to get married again – as usual. (I'm still looking for that girl I said I was going to find.)

There are very few shortages here that we used to hear about. You can still get good steak dinners, Johnny Walker

Scotch, good bourbon, black market gas, etc. About the only two things that were hard to get are tires and cigarettes. Even the PX's limit cigarettes to two packs per man. Everything considered, however, the U.S. is a great place to be and I am damned glad to be back. People have been swell to returners and by people, I mean both civilians and military men.

Field grade officers are classified and assigned out of Washington, my assignment turning out to be Second Air Force HQ here at Colorado Springs. I arrived to find that now I will be reassigned from here to some 2nd AF unit and that is what I am sweating out now. This is a hell of a spot to be waiting with Christmas only three days away. I haven't seen many familiar faces around here – I guess they are all in B 29's which is probably where I will be. They certainly are putting the pressure on the extra heavies. General Travis is back from U.K. and is in command of the 17th Wing again – now the Second Air Force can operate again!!

Have been reading quite a bit about the 15th AF raids so I know that the Wing is hard at it with plans Able, Baker, Charlie, Dog, Easy, Fox, George, How, etc. Boy, what a nightmare that is. It is such a swell outfit though, that no work is really hard. I know I will never run into a finer bunch of men than are in the 304th Wing and were in the 99th BG. It can't be a coincidence that they were both commanded by the same man.

One of my first impressions of public attitude toward the war was that war was all over with. There was really a pronounced complacency which showed up in radio, press and ordinary conversation. The present German counter-drive is really changing that attitude now, but it is a damned shame that lessons have to be learned at such a terrific cost. The public is getting a rude awakening, but they are taking it well. The general feeling now is – "why those dirty bastards – they can't do that to us." That is the feeling and I think now production will be on the upgrade again. This war is certainly in a mess now – setbacks in Europe, internal war in Greece and disagreements among the Allies. It's a great life.

I guess I have wandered on in this letter long enough, General, so I'll put my flaps down and call it a day. A belated Merry Christmas to you and all the boys in Wg. HQ. The very best of luck--

Sincerely,
/s/ Harry Burrell

P.S. Hello to Col. Cool, Col. Krauss, Williams, Thompson, Doc, Kolpin, Moose, McGarrity, Large and all the rest. If you can find a spare moment, General, I sure would like to hear how things are. Address: 5002 Parker Street Omaha, Nebraska

4 January 1945

Dear Gen. Upthegrove:

This letter is being written from Galveston, Texas, which I am convinced, is a reunion point for the old 99th Bomb Group. If I were to put a list here of the men at this base, it would sound like a roster of the 99th. Doyle and Flex arrived today and like myself, are going to go through this standardization school. Jim Hager, Bill Mehew, Bob Elliott, Bankhead, T.J. Davis, and Bob Copsey are all instructors here and practically the entire 99th has been through here. Right now we are all reminiscing and wishing that you could be here to take us all overseas again in B 29's. We decided to write this round-robin letter so I will turn this over to the next man. The best of luck, General ---

H. R. Burrell

Dear General:

Not being a drinking man, this scotch and Seagrams has almost done me in. I was planning to write you as soon as I knew what the score was. But I guess I'll write you while they still have us mixed up. You sure can't figure out what goes on in the minds of the people back here in the states.

The only way I would enjoy going overseas again is to have you as our leader plus a few good men who made the great "99th". Such as Harry, George and a few others.

Best of luck to you General – (The best officer and boss in the Air Forces) and also to all of our friends in the 304th. Here is Georgie!

J. S. Flex

Dear General:

Well, sir, since leaving Italy this is my first assignment. What a wonderful surprise to find so many of the old 99th boys here. Bob Elliott has a new baby boy.

Erickson and Shelby of the 348th are here. In fact, Bankhead is the only one that I haven't seen as yet.

All the boys ask for you. They all think so highly of you and say so many nice things about you that I feel that I just have to set them straight on a few things. How about that?

We're all sweating out the future. Why don't you come back and form a real good outfit.

Now that I have an address I'll write you. My best to you and all the boys of the 304th.

George (Coen)

Dear Sir,

I don't know quite what to say but first of all I want to give you congratulations on your promotion. I don't believe that their were three happier men than Jim Hager, Bob Elliott and myself. May I wish the best for all three of us.

Jim, Bob and I have been here instructing for the last 10 months, but it looks as though we will be going over before long. I'm almost ready to have my nerve worked up in order to be checked out in a B-24, so that I may get in your wing. I hope I last that long.

I'll turn this over to Hager, so in case you have time to answer this, just address it:

Capt. Bill R. Mehew
202nd I I U. - A.A.B.
Galveston, Texas

Dear Uppie:

Since we're all drunk we all love you. Met a buddy of yours – Gen. McGinnis speaks very well of you. The drunker we get, the more this can go on, so I'll sign off now.

Please write when you get time.

As ever,
Jim Hager

Photo, Courtesy of Mrs. W.R. Burrell

Colonel Harry R. Burrell

Colonel Burrell was the Commander at Langley Air Force Base, Virginia when this photo was taken. He was up for Brigadier General at the time he died of lymph cancer in June, 1966. He was buried with honors at Arlington National Cemetery, a short distance from the Tomb of The UNKNOWN SOLDIER.

A TRIBUTE TO CAPTAIN HARRY BURRELL

No one paid a higher tribute to Harry Burrell than that repeated many times by General Upthegrove. "If I had a son, I would have wanted him to be like Harry". He wrote me these words in much of our correspondence. The General, the Bankheads,and my wife and I had daughters.

The 99th moved to Italy as I was getting ready for my return to the States. Harry completed his 50th mission from the base in Italy and then stayed on to work in Operations for General Upthegrove. On his return to the States he got out of the Air Corps for a short time. Being a civilian did not suit him and he became a member of the regular army upon receiving a recommendation from General Upthegrove.

Harry was also a SAC commander in the U.S. and England. The English people loved him and the press carried glowing reports about what a great Commander he was. The NEWBURY WEEKLY NEWS sent me many news stories about Harry and have been waiting for the book I told them I was undertaking.

Back in the States, Harry was called upon to pilot a Strato-tanker from New York to London to try for a speed record. The third plane that was to follow crashed on take off. Harry reached London before he learned of the tragedy.

The tanker that crashed is described here in the Friday, June 27, 1958 edition of the OMAHA WORLD HERALD release:

JET TANKER'S BID FOR RECORD ENDS IN TRAGEDY AS 15 KILLED

A giant Air Force jet tanker's bid for a speed record ended in death for 15 persons early Friday, seconds after departure from Westover Air Force Base, Mass. The tanker, one of four attempting to set speed records across the Atlantic Ocean, tangled with a high-tension wire, skidded across the

Massachusetts Turnpike and burst into flames. The dead included Brig. Gen. Donald W. Saunders, commander of the Fifty-seventh Air Division, airborne commander of the flight; Lieut. Col. George M. Broutsas, aircraft commander; James McGonaughy, Jr., chief of the Washington Bureau of Time-Life; and Robert A. Ginsburgh, retired Air Force brigadier general and associate editor of U.S. News and World Report.

Harry returned from London to NEW YORK in record time of 5 1/2 hours two days later. He was met by Lt. General Francis Griswold on his return. General Griswold was the Deputy Commander of SAC under General Curtiss Le May. The Associated Press wire photo was sent to me by them for inclusion here.

Photo - Courtesy of OMAHA WORLD HERALD. June 28, 1958

SPEEDSTERS WELCOMED BACK

Col. Harry R. Burrell, of Omaha, Nebraska, Flight Commander, salutes Lt. General Francis H. Griswold, left, Vice Commander of The Strategic Air Command, as he descends from a KC 135 Jet Tanker after setting the East - to - West flight record. At right is Major Burl Davenport of San Antonio, Texas, pilot of the plane called ALPHA flown in the operation.

Elapsed time for the 3,460 mile flight from London, England, was 5 hours, 51 minutes, and 24.8 seconds.

Here reprinted by permission of the Omaha World Herald is the account of the record breaking flight.

OMAHA WORLD HERALD - JUNE 30, 1958

JET TANKERS CLIP RECORD

Omahan Didn't Know of Crash Fatal to 15

New York (ap) - Two United States Air Force jet tanker planes flew from London to New York Saturday in the record time of less than six hours, more than an hour and a half faster than the old mark.

The same craft had set marks of less than 5 1/2 hours for the New York-London flight only two days ago.

The British held the previous records of 7 hours 29 minutes on a London to New York flight and 6 hours 16 minutes from New York to London.

3rd Plane Crashed

The first of the two Air Force planes - the Alpha-flashed over the Idlewild Airport at 1:20 p.m. to complete the 3,460 mile trans-atlantic flight in 5 hours, 51 minutes.

The Alpha's sister ship, the Bravo, arrived two minutes later.

Four of the planes — KC-135 'a — had been scheduled to make the round trip flight to England. The Alpha and the Bravo got away safely but the third plane crashed with the loss of 15 lives. Six newsmen were among them. The flight of the fourth craft was then canceled.

Col. Harry Burrell of Omaha, 40 year old commander of the flight, told newsmen upon landing that those aboard the Alpha and Bravo didn't learn of the crash until they reached England.

It has been mistakenly understood previously that the plane commanders had been told.

Colonel Burrell said the absence of any communication from the other two ships scheduled for the hop did not lead to any speculation. But "each of us privately wondered perhaps," he added.

Flew at 26,000

The Alpha averaged 587.72 m.p.h. for the flight from London to New York. It bettered by 17 minutes its estimated time of arrival here.

Colonel Burrell said:

"We did a little better than we expected. We had good tail winds over Maine and out of Ireland," he said.

They flew at 26 thousand feet.

Major Quenton W. Raaz, of Jefferson, Iowa, piloted Bravo.

From the three large scrapbooks shown me by Harry's Mother, a book of some 100 pages could be written.

When I went to Omaha to work on storm duty for an insurance adjusting company, I was not aware that Harry had died of cancer. When I called his mother, I fully expected she would give me his present address. His passing was written up in England with much praise in his work he had accomplished while commanding the SAC unit there. Their article is worth mentioning here.

FORMER AIR BASE COMMANDER DIES

Here reprinted through the courtesy of the NEWBURY WEEKLY NEWS is a story those who loved Harry will be pleased to read.

Many local residents will regret to hear to of the death on June 24, after a long illness, of Col. Harry R. Burrell, who commanded the United States 3909th Air Base Group at Greenham Common from 1954 to 1957. Only 48 years of age, he rose through the ranks of the Army Air Corps as a B-17 pilot to become a bomb squadron commander in North Africa, an operations officer of a bomb wing in Italy and an air inspector at Harvard Army Air Base, Neb. During the last war he flew, as pilot, 50 combat missions in 308 combat hours, and received outstanding high decorations. On leaving Greenham in August, 1957, he held more important commands in the United States. He leaves a wife, Shirley, and three children.

Wholehearted co-operation

When base commander at Greenham, Col. Burrell tried by every conceivable means to avoid upsetting local people through aircraft disturbance. When the base became fully operational with the big six-jet B47 bombers, he drew up a tight schedule of do's and don'ts for his men. Subject to service exigencies, he banned flying during church services, prohibited flying over the town, cut down night operations and when planes had to be tested, placed them in special positions as far from houses as possible. On his suggestion, the then Mayor formed a committee of representatives of various town interests to co-operate with the U.S. Officers in tackling kindred problems.

A great ambassador

This fine gesture of good neighborliness was warmly appreciated. But the colonel went one further. A family man himself, he thought of the local children, and arranged a special day for them, invited parents to bring their under-14s to Greenham to see the huge planes at rest. His idea was that if kiddies saw the aircraft grounded and silent, they would be more likely to accept them as an every-day feature of life and would not be so frightened when they roared across the skies. Hundreds turned up, were allowed to look over the jets, watched take-offs and demonstrations and had everything explained to them. Col. Burrell was undoubtedly one of his country's best ambassadors.

Members of the 99th Bomb Group and the SAC members will agree that Col. Harry Burrell was one of the great Heroes of the War.

COLONEL HARRY R. BURRELL

Colonel Harry R. Burrell was the SAC Commander at the RAF station at Greenham Common, England in 1957. He laid the corner-stone for the new Chapel there on March 25, 1957. The cornerstone is inscribed:

THIS STONE WAS LAID BY
COLONEL HARRY R. BURRELL
BASE COMMANDER
MCMLVII

When Colonel Burrell returned to the US the Town held a dinner in his honor. From her three scrapbooks, his mother furnished this great tribute to him by the English people:

GREENHAM AIR BASE LOSING ITS NO. 1 DIPLOMAT

TOWN LUNCH FOR COL. BURRELL

A lunch in honor of Col. Harry R. Burrell, U.S.A.F. Base Commander at Greenham Common, prior to his return to America early next month at the end of his overseas assignment, was given by the Mayor (Councillor M.W. Paine), at the Chequers on Friday.

The Mayor presided, others present being the Mayoress (Miss Dora Paine), Lord and Lady Teviot, Lord and Lady Porchester, Councillor and Mrs. R. J. Huckle, Councillor and Mrs. F. P. Pirouet, Councillor and Mrs. G. E. Willis, Mr. and

Mrs. Frank Howes, Col. E. J. S. Ward, Mr. and Mrs. Leslie Southern, Mr. T. J. Fisher, Col. W. R Yancey, Col. and Mrs. A. S. Cresswell and Wing-Commander and Mrs. J. G. Lingard.

Flags of the two nations, hung between a large replica of the Borough Coat of Arms, were a feature of the decorations.

Tried To Minimize Difficulties

The Mayor said an endeavor had been made to invite to the lunch a fair representation of local people who had been closely associated with Col. Burrell during his term of service at Greenham. Among those unable to accept were Mr. and Mrs. Anthony Hurd. The Mayor warmly welcomed Col. Cresswell, who is to be the new base commander, and of Col. Burrell said the town and district would be losing a very sympathetic and understanding friend, who by his co-operation, unfailing courtesy and good humour had done all he could to minimize the difficulties and grievances caused by having jet bombers on Newbury's doorstep. They greatly appreciated his work and recognized that the Americans had really done their best to be good neighbors. They wished God-speed to Col. and Mrs. Burrell when they returned to the States.

Came at Unhappy Time

Councillor R. J. Huckle, proposing a toast to their "Guest of Honor" said Colonel Burrell assumed command at Greenham Common three years ago just after the occasion that could perhaps best be described as the time of the rude awakening. "We had recovered to some extent from the extreme sense of loss that we experienced when some hundreds of acres of our most cherished common land was converted to military purposes, and suddenly we had been brought to the grim realization that the serenity of our delightful countryside was in danger of being completely assigned to the Greenham

Common for operational training purposes," he continued. The position had been further aggravated by the publicity given to some ill-considered criticisms of local hospitality made by a U.S. sergeant, who in addition to having stripes on his jacket appeared to be carrying a chip on each shoulder.

Sympathetic and Understanding

"The occasion then demanded a man of outstanding ability, possessed of imagination, tact, and a sympathetic understanding of our difficulties," continued Councillor Huckler. "In Col. Burrell we were delighted to find such a man. A splendid example of his imaginative approach to our problems was when he invited all the children of the neighborhood and their mothers to the base in order that they could make friends with the bombers that were causing all the unrest." That Col. Burrell had also sympathy and understanding was proved by the diplomatic way in which he had handled every complaint, however trivial made to him, and there had been dozens of such complaints.

But apart from his official position, Col. Burrell would best be remembered for the way in which he and his charming wife had submerged themselves completely into our local life. They made the perfect partnership, experiencing the English character in all its aspects, attending functions in town or village and lending to the proceedings their quiet dignity or subtle gaiety as the occasion demanded. Interesting themselves in everything and meeting all kinds of people they had forged new links of friendship.

Had Newbury's Goodwill

Describing the function as probably the nicest thing that had ever happened to him, Col. Burrell said his wife and himself were deeply touched by the honor accorded them. He especially appreciated the concrete evidence of goodwill shown them and would like everyone to know how much they appreciated the wholehearted co-operation they had always received not only from those present at the lunch but from the entire local community. No partnership was a success unless there was mutual respect and understanding, there must be give and take and by their combined efforts he felt that in some measure they had contributed to a better understanding between their two countries.

"Shirley and I will never forget the friends we have made here in Newbury and district during these three years; it has been a wonderful and rewarding experience. We wish you all good luck, good health and God bless you," concluded the Colonel.

Captain H. Blaine Bankhead

Truly, onc of the first Heroes of the 99th Bomb Group.
Now, retired Captain of Delta Airlines.
(Residing Peachtree City, GA.)

H.B. (BUD) BANKHEAD

H. B. (Bud) Bankhead became my first pilot and I his co-pilot early in our transition training. Captain Harry Burrell became operations officer and had to relinquish the crew he hand picked. He told me that he chose Bankhead who was a great pilot. He should know as he checked out all the First pilots in our group.

We were both 24 years of age. Bankhead had gone to College while I had only a few semesters at the University of Wisconsin Extension Division in Milwaukee. Throughout my entire training, no one ever asked me what college or university I had graduated from.

Bankhead's home town newspaper provides a good profile of him that is reprinted here. I must add that we have kept in touch every year since our return from combat. Our families grew up together by mail. Irene and I had two daughters. A son died eight hours after birth in 1956. Bankhead married a lovely stewardess when flying for Chicago-Southern Airlines. The Airline later merged with Delta Air Lines. Bankhead was one of their top pilots and was flying the wide body L-1011 at the time he reached retirement age.

PROMINENT WELLSVILLE FLIER MISSING IN NORTH AFRICA

First Lieutenant Heber Blaine "Bud" Bankhead, only son of Mr. and Mrs. Heber H. Bankhead of Wellsville, was today reported missing in the North African war theater since May 25.

The telegram, received by his parents and reported by Mayor LaMont Allen, read as follows: "The war department regrets to inform you that the commanding general of the North African area reports your son, First Lieutenant Heber Blaine Bankhead, missing in action since May 25.

If further details of his status are received, you will be notified."

Well known in Cache valley athletic circles, and a graduate in agriculture and dairy manufacturing from Utah State Agricultural college in 1940 Lieutenant Bankhead was first pilot of a Flying Fortress.

In a letter received last night by his folks and dated May 23 - two days before he was lost - he stated he had been on 15 bombing raids and "was still going strong." Blaine was well liked and admired by all who knew him, and an excellent softball player before he joined the army.

Born April 20, 1918, in Wellsville, he is a son of Heber H. and Margaret Williamson Bankhead. He was graduated from South Cache High School in 1936, and from the USAC in 1940. Enlisting in the air corps July 1941, he trained at Bakers Field, Oxnard and Mather Field, Cal., receiving his wings at the Sacramento field in January 1942. Then he went to Craig Field, Ala., and Spence Field, Ga., as flight instructor. At Hendricks Field, Fla., he was promoted to first lieutenant and made first pilot of a B-17.

Prior to flying overseas in February of 1943 he served at Gowen Field, Idaho; Walla Walla, Wash.; Sioux City, Iowa and Salina, Kansas.

Besides his parents he has two sisters, Ruth Bankhead, instructor at South Cache High, and Lorraine Bankhead, all of Wellsville.

Bankhead was awarded the D.F.C. for the Messina mission. I still felt he earned the Silver Star as I was the one beside him when he handled the B-17 as if he was in Single engine advanced training and instruction at Maxwell, Ala. He went to four-engine bombers from there. This award was given after the ordeal of the Messina mission.

CAPTAIN EDMUND JANIC
Bombardier Hero of World War II

Edmund Janic was one of the first High School graduates to pass the rigid three day college test for candidates without 60 college credits.

Appointment to U.S. Army Flying Cadet Training followed successful completion of test.

A TRIBUTE TO CAPTAIN EDDIE JANIC

I worked with Ed Janic during the 1940's on construction in the city of Milwaukee. Our employer, Dahlmann Construction was good to us and found inside jobs during the winter for the men. It was Eddie who suggested that we get into the Aviation Cadets and learn to fly. While he passed the three day college test on his first try in 1940, it was September of 1941, after my third try that I finally made it. Eddie became a bombardier after Pearl Harbor as he had washed himself out of Primary training when his father took ill. Eddie came home and was the sole support of the family.

He distinguished himself in the Eighth Air Force in England and was decorated many times. Lord Tranchard of the Royal Air Force Command commended him for this expertise and courage in his determination to get the bombs on target.His B-24 Liberator group also made trips to Africa also on their way to bomb the Ploesti Oil Fields. One of my classmates, Captain Black was in his group. Reprinted here is a press release his sister, Marie Devereaux gave me when we met to discuss my project in writing this book.

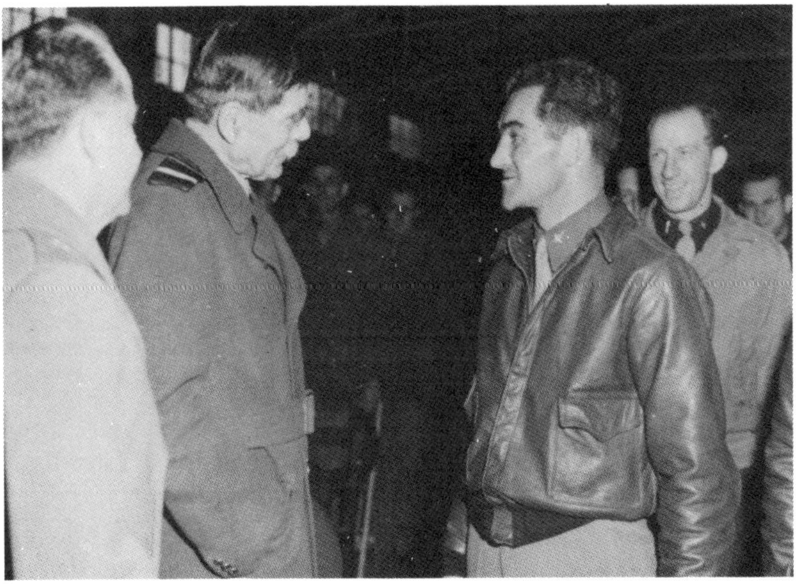

Photo - Courtesy of Mrs. Marie Devereau

CAPTAIN EDMUND JANIC, in flight jacket speaks with LORD TRANCHARD of the RAF upon return from a harrowing mission to Germany.

AIRMAN TELLS OF A WILD RIDE IN BOMBER ABOUT TO EXPLODE

A wild ride from Tunisia to Malta in a Liberator bomber that was about to explode in midair was related by Lieut. Edmund Janic, 3757 S. Kansas Ave., and his crewmates in a "Stars and Stripes in Britain" broadcast from England Tuesday. Lieut. Janic was bombardier on the American bomber "Shoot Luke, " which was traveling what pilots call "the old milk route" over Tunisia. Returning from a bombing of Scusse Jan. 19, "Shoot Luke" and several companion craft were furiously attacked by Axis fighter planes. The "Shoot Luke's" gunners shot down three of the foe, but the ship suffered a hit from an explosive shell that seriously wounded two crew members.

Lieut. Janic related how he left his station in the ship's nose to bandage the wounded men and to keep the commander posted on fires and damage. Nearing Malta for an emergency landing, the crew noticed smoke and flame licking at the fuselage. The ship landed with no trouble, but the crew found on inspection that had they remained in the air five minutes longer the "Shoot Luke" would have been blown to bits. Three of her gasoline compartments were ablaze.

News reached Milwaukee April 12 that Lieut. Janic had been decorated, but details of his exploits were not given. Nor did Tuesday's broadcast indicate whether the "Shoot Luke" incident had been so rewarded.

My last letter from Eddie was received when I was at Fort Worth, Texas. He was at Fitzsimmons General Hospital. I never grasped the bloody bugs bit, but was to learn later that he had contracted malaria. His letter follows:

November 9, 1944

Capt. James F. Bruno
Ft. Worth A.A.F. O.S.D.
Ft. Worth, Texas

Dear Jim,

It was a pleasant surprise to hear from you Congratulations on the coming heir.

As you know, the bloody bugs bit me and now I've got nothing but sack time trying to get rid of them. I've been here about a month and a half now and I'll wager I've spent 99% on my back.

I don't know whether you know it or not but we were both at Tafaroui, outside Oran on the same day. You were in the 99th weren't you? Any hoo, we pulled in there in the morning from the Middle East on our way back to England, and I guess you people were just coming over to put a finish to that nasty old war.

By the way, I fought the war with a chum of yours, George G. Black. He came down to see me in September at Muroc. He had just returned from England. He and I were great buddies and we had some lovely times together. He too, is a Captain and was assigned to a gunnery school at Laredo, Texas. I haven't heard from him since, but I will when he gets settled down and it happens to rain for a week in a row.

Jackson, I'm fresh out of nonsense. Thanks for writing and if you can manage, write again.

CU

ED

Capt. Edmund F. Janic 0661000
Ward C-2
Fitzsimmons General Hospital
Denver, 8 Colorado

I was out of the service and operating at the Waukesha County Airport when I was notified that Eddie had died. His sister, Marie gave me the Milwaukee Journal write-up. I attended the funeral service at the Cathedral and then went to the airport to fly over St. Adalbert's Cemetery during the burial service. I had lost one of the best friends a man could ask for.

CAPTAIN JANIC, 29, LONG ILL, DIES

One of the City's War Heroes

Ill for more than a year, Capt. Edmund F. Janic, 29, son of Mr. and Mrs. Anthony Janic, 3757 S. Kansas Ave., died Tuesday at the Fitzsimmons general hospital, Denver, Col., relatives were informed Wednesday. One of the city's heroes of the war, Capt. Janic held the silver star, the Purple Heart, the distinguished flying cross and the air medal with three oak leaf clusters. He took part in the famous raid on the Ploesti oil fields in Rumania. In March, 1943, he was wounded in a raid on Nazi occupied Europe. He took part in more than 35 missions.

A graduate of Marquette high school, Capt. Janic qualified as a flying cadet in 1941 even though he had never been to college. He was the first Milwaukee high school graduate to pass the examination, according to army authorities.

Besides his parents, he is survived by a brother, Ray, a seaman, second class, stationed at Norman, Okla., and three sisters, Eleanor, Mrs. Marie Devereaux and Mrs. Blanche Zablocki.

Funeral services will be held at 10 a.m. Saturday at St. Vincent de Paul church. Burial will be in St. Adalbert 's cemetery.

CHAPTER 18

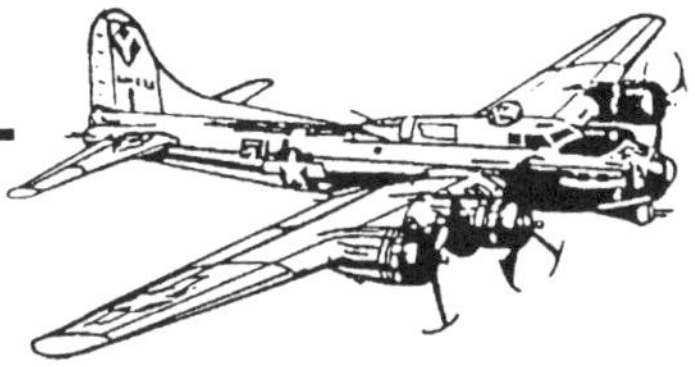

The Air Force Reserve

While working in the City of Wausau, WI, a Lieutenant Colonel who operated a sporting goods store, together with an Air Force Major, came up with the plan to form a Reserve training unit for Wausau and the surrounding communities. This was acceptable to me. Within our social group were fighter pilots, navigators, gunners and bombardiers. Given a few planes, we could support a small war of our own.

In January, 1949, about 25 men formed the 9663rd Volunteer Air Reserve Training Unit. The War having ended only five years earlier, we were eager to experience some flying again. Being a Captain, I accepted the position of Statistical Officer. Later, I was promoted to Operations and Training. It was a far cry from my Operations and Training position at Ellington Field near Houston, Texas.

One day, the "Brass" decided we should be paid for our meeting attendance. Senator Joseph McCarthy was contacted by our Lieutenant Colonel and flew to Wausau via Wisconsin Central Airlines. The meeting was held at the Wausau Hotel in a room reserved for us. As we sat down, Senator McCarthy informed us he had ordered drinks to be sent to the room. That announcement provided a more relaxed atmosphere for all present.

Our Lieutenant Colonel made the plea for our members to receive compensation for the weekend meetings. Senator Mc Carthy, knowing his reputation in Washington for alluding to Communists in government, told us frankly, "I am not the fair-haired boy there but I will do what I can for all of you." We felt we had chosen someone to go to bat for us and were at the airport to see him off to D.C. About six years later our wishes came true. Some of our pilots were fortunate enough to fly the F-80 Lockheed out of Minneapolis.

In March of 1951, my company transferred me to Detroit, Michigan where I joined their Reserve unit. The Reserves were allowed to fly the F-86 out of Selfridge Field, Michigan. In February of 1951, I had been promoted to Major in the Reserve and the monthly check for that grade bought groceries for a week. However, I did not qualify for flying as a 1958 physical reported my left ear was showing a 55% hearing loss. I was grounded.

It did not apply to my civilian pilot license which allowed me to rent planes occasionally when finances permitted.

Many ex-service pilots I was acquainted with wanted nothing to do with flying or the Reserves. With all of their experience and over a thousand hours of military flying I could not understand what could turn them off on flying. Many people would give anything to be able to go into the air given their license and experience.

In 1954, a promotion to Branch Office Manager in Northern Michigan was offered to me. The Branch Manager there wanted to transfer to Grand Rapids so he could continue his

Army Reserve training which was not available at his present location. As a result of my accepting the promotion, I left the training unit in Detroit. A group of servicemen did suggest that we drive 60 miles north to Traverse City, Michigan to join their unit but that never materialized. So it was to the Standby Reserve in Denver.

Two years later I returned to Milwaukee, Wisconsin and became active in the Reserve again. Once again, I was transferred to Wausau as Branch Manager and rejoined the Reserve unit I had helped form.

I received a letter from the 10th Air Force at Wausau suggesting that Majors and above could apply for a seminar given by the Industrial College of The Armed Forces. I applied to serve as a representative for the Insurance Industry. I was put on orders and spent a very informative ten days at the seminar. Army, Air Force and Navy instructors gave us information not made public or known to anyone who had not attended the War College.

One astonishing fact told us was about a book written in 1904 by an Englishman named Sir Malford Mackinder. He drew a map showing the World Island. The European Islands, Russia and Asia were shown as the Marginal Crescent which constituted the Heartland. Africa and the Middle East were also within the boundaries of the land mass called the World Island. Mackinder reasoned that he who ruled the Heartland ruled the Continent. Then, he who ruled the Continent ruled the World Island. Therefore, he who ruled the World Island, ruled the World.

In 1923, Rudolph Hess brought a visitor to the Landsberg jail. He was Major General Rudolph Haushofer. He came to visit Corporal Adolph Hitler. General Haushofer brought with him the book Mackinder had written in 1904. That book and its theory caused Hitler to write a new chapter in the book, "Mein Kampf" he was writing. Germany, he wrote, "would be

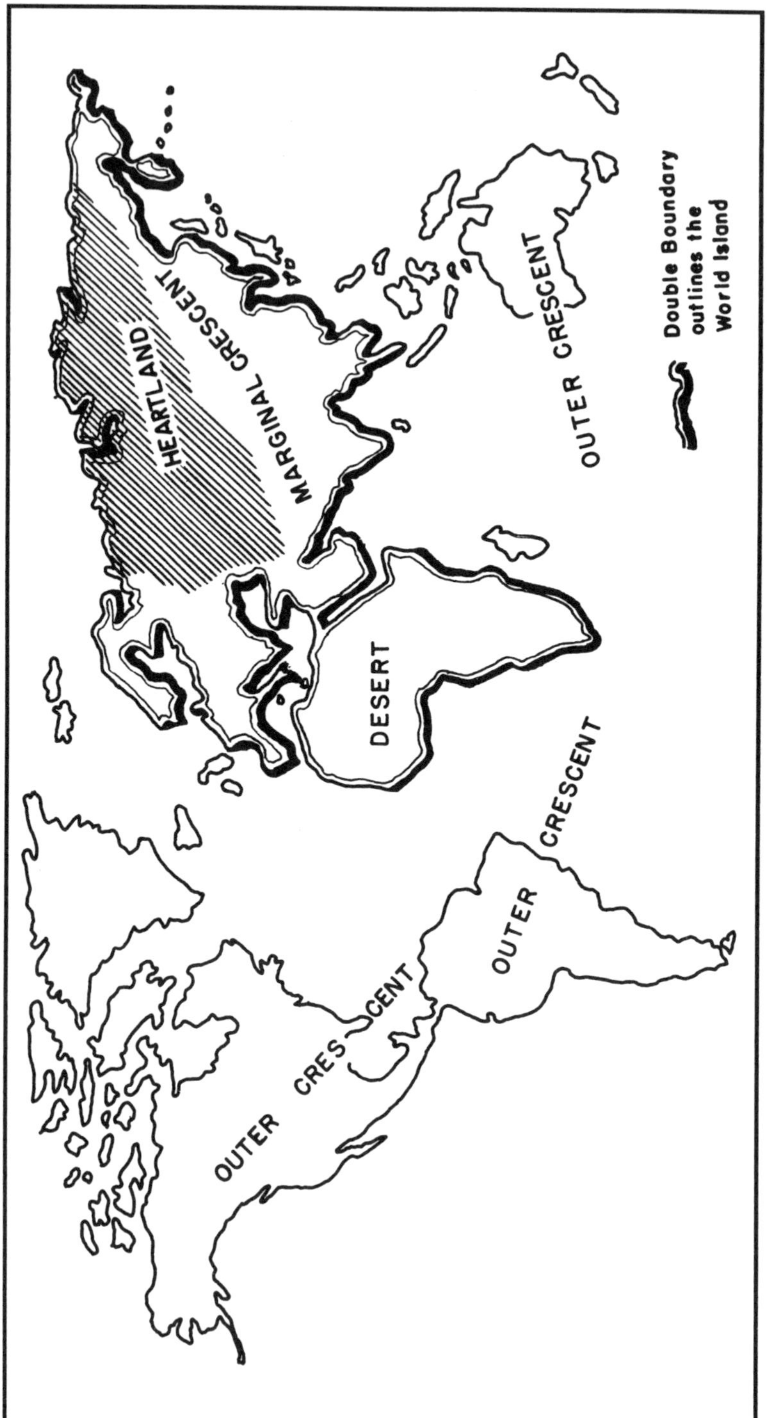

Mackinder's Map of the World (1904)

a world power, or not at all." Ten years later, in 1933, Hitler began his rise to power.

As for General Haushofer, he was to begin the College of Geo-politics in Munich which was attended by the Japanese, the Italians and all German officers. Geopolitics was the study of Geography, History and Political Theory. In his book, Mackinder wrote the Heartland was the Russian continent which contained seven-eights of the population and the bulk of the continent's raw materials. It was this prize Hitler envisioned for Germany.

Another amazing and stirring revelation came when an Army Colonel opened his speech with the words, "America will spend itself into destruction." Those words, he stated, were uttered by Soviet Premier Nikita Kruschev in 1954 to the Russian Parliament. The Communists, he stated, would start a series of small actions or wars to draw the United States into them. The Army Colonel further stated these facts were known and communicated to the men in the Pentagon, the President and his Security Cabinet.

Almost ten years after this boast by Kruschev, President Lyndon Johnson ordered our men into Vietnam over a minor P.T. Boat incident. This was the war France had warned our country not to become involved with.

Nations Business, in their March, 1974 issue, carried an article by Dr. William Peterson, Professor of American Business at the Graduate School of International Management, Glendale, Arizona, which stated that U. S. involvement in Vietnam resulted in 46,000 combat deaths, 300,000 Combat wounded. The United States sustained $135 Billion of turmoil at home strongly shaking the terms of two Presidents.

Robert S. McNamara with whom I had the opportunity to become one of his Whiz Kids mentioned in a previous chapter, has come out with a book in 1995 confessing the "Sins of Vietnam."

As early as February, 1952 at the seminar given by the Industrial College of The Armed Forces we learned the Communists were going to start a series of small wars and that America would enter them and "Spend itself into Destruction".

Where were President Lyndon Johnson and Secretary of War, Robert McNamara when the warning was given nine years before?

While the war protestors flung the epithet,"Murderer" at McNamara, I was to hear it, too, from my University of Minnesota student, my daughter, Diana. I was in the Air Force Reserve to fulfill my retirement pay obligations. I did not relish being called a murderer because of that. I knew and I was sure they both were making a grave mistake.

Daughter Diana born in Houston, Texas April 26, 1945.
When The Vietnam War was entered into by the U.S., Diana was three and one half years into her degree at the University of Minnesota. She quit the University and became a war protester.

On the other hand, my daughter quit the university after three and one half years to join the protesters and traveled to San Francisco living with the "hippies " in the Haight-Ashbury district.

My entire family became a Victim of that war. It broke up a caring family living in the upscale Linden Hills area in south Minneapolis.

Vietnam was not our War!

MEMO: I was in the 440th Troop Carrier in Milwaukee on Reserve duty when I discovered why the Air Corps wanted to send me to Dayton, Ohio. This was one week after the FBI was convinced I was not spying for the Germans.

Unwisely, I requested the officer to give some other pilot the assignment.

EX-AF CAPTAIN IS NEW DOD CHIEF

Washington (AFPS) - Robert S. McNamara, president of the Ford Motor Co. and a former Air Force lieutenant colonel, has been named Secretary of Defense by President-elect John F. Kennedy. Mr. McNamara has been with the Ford Co. since 1946. His appointment as Defense Department chief came only a month after his election to the presidency of Ford.

A native of San Francisco, Mr. McNamara won Phi Beta Kappa honors in his sophomore year at the University of California. He was graduated in 1937. Two years later he received his master's degree from the Harvard School of Business Administration.

After 11 years with an accounting firm on the West Coast, Mr. McNamara returned to Harvard as an assistant professor of business administration. On a leave of absence he joined the War Department to help build a statistical control system for the Army Air Corps. This program was later applied to the whole logistics operation of the Air Force.

During WWII, Mr. McNamara was commissioned a captain in the Air Force, serving in England, India, China and the Pacific. He was awarded the Legion of Merit and by the time of his discharge had risen to the rank of lieutenant colonel.

(During the war Mr. McNamara and nine other young officers worked as a team at Wright Field, Dayton, Ohio, revolutionizing Air Corps procurement and supply through new methods of statistical control. The team stayed together after the war and joined the Ford Motor Co. in 1945.)

Mr. McNamara is an avid and experienced mountain climber. Another of his favorite pastimes is skiing. He lives with his wife and three children in Ann Arbor, Michigan.

THE INDUSTRIAL COLLEGE OF ARMED FORCES

The week I was selected to attend the seminar, my company decided my services were no longer needed at the Wausau office. The Milwaukee headquarters also informed me the state had no other openings available to me.

After a request to fill a Branch Manager's vacancy in Northern Michigan once again, I accepted. Two years later, I returned to Wisconsin.

I was in the Reserves a year when I came up for promotion to Lt. Colonel. I was notified by the Promotion Board I had missed too many years of continuous service in the Reserve and they had no recourse except to discharge me back to a civilian.

The discharge did give me the option to rejoin the Reserve program as an enlisted man with the rank of Airman First Class. After deliberating with my wife, I became an Airman First Class.

The Majors and some other ranking officers whom I outranked by date of service (September, 1942) were now my superiors. Those two stripes did not match too well with my Silver wings and Campaign ribbons. Nevertheless, I wore them proudly, even when I was pulling KP in the serving line. For seven years I served in the enlisted ranks and made Staff Sergeant and later Tech. Sergeant. I became a Command Post Specialist at the Minneapolis troop carrier unit. They were able to pass the annual inspection by the Air Force due to my Command Post charts and my up-to-date knowledge of them.

Upon my moving to Milwaukee again, the Minneapolis unit had another base inspection coming up. No other enlisted man was qualified to handle the Command Post part of the inspection. They offered to fly to Milwaukee to have me come up to help them pass the test. I took the Greyhound bus instead and they passed with flying colors. Their Base Commander had been a fighter pilot and I always had the best of rapport with him. It was a pleasure working in his unit. I went to a two weeks active duty with his unit in Alaska. They outperformed the group unit of which they were one squadron.

Finally, in 1970, I had completed twenty good years for retirement purposes. I again reverted to my rank of Major since my Officer service had exceeded ten years.

CHAPTER 19

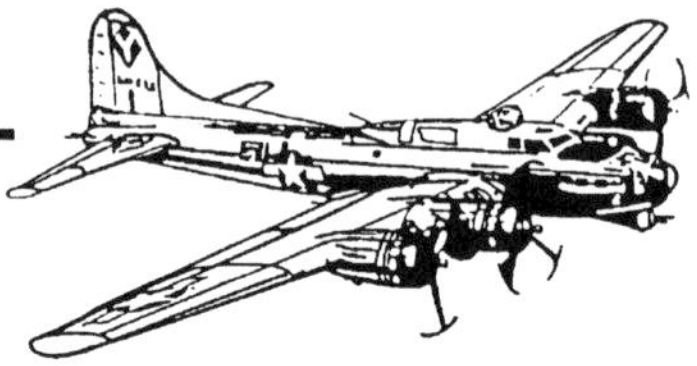

THE 99th BOMB GROUP HISTORICAL SOCIETY

The 99th Bomb Group Historical Society is one of many which have been organized since the early 1950's. Credit goes to our George Coen, Walter Butler and Bernie Barr, all hailing from Albuquerque, New Mexico. Through their efforts, men were recruited to join the fledgling organization, now over 800 strong.

I first heard of the Society in 1981 when my best friend and first pilot, H. Blaine Bankhead, wrote to me about it. I joined shortly thereafter.

The next reunion was held at Muskegon, Michigan. It was close to home for me as my wife and I lived across Lake Michigan in Waukesha, Wisconsin. I sent my reservations in early and eagerly looked forward to meeting the men I had not seen since leaving Africa in November, 1943.

My wife, Irene, had undergone cancer surgery six months prior to the scheduled reunion. Due to resulting complications our plans to attend were canceled. On September 12, 1985 my beautiful wife lost her courageous battle with cancer.

In June of 1986, I made a reservation for another reunion.

The Dedication of our 99th Memorial occurred at Dayton, Ohio with over 450 members and wives attending.

The following year the Group met in Dallas, Texas.

Each reunion stands out in our memories due to the enduring and indivisible bond forged amongst us in the African Campaign.

Here is a list of those memorable reunions from 1957 to 1995.

REUNION LOCATIONS

1.		1957	Sioux City, IA
2.		1959	Chicago, IL
3.		1961	Chicago, IL
4.	Oct.	1980	Amarillo, TX
5.	Apr.	1981	Albuquerque, NM
6.	July	1981	Rapid City, SD
7.	Apr.	1982	Albuquerque, NM
8.	Oct.	1982	Muskegon, MI
9.	May	1983	Albuquerque, NM
10.	May	1984	Houston, TX
11.	July	1985	Seattle, WA
12.	June	1986	Dayton, OH
13.	Apr.	1987	Dallas, TX
14.	Oct.	1987	Colorado Springs, CO
15.	June	1988	Fort Lauderdale, FL
16.	Feb.	1989	McAllen, TX
17.	Apr.	1990	Huntsville, AL
18.	Sept.	1991	Albuquerque, NM
19.	Sept.	1992	Rapid City, SD
20.	Oct.	1993	Ontario, CA
21.	Sept.	1994	Hampton, VA
22.	May	1995	St. Louis, MO

Memorial Plaque
Air Force Museum, Dayton, Ohio

The above plaque honoring those of us who served with the 99th Bomb Group can be seen on the memorial grounds near the Air Force Museum.

The dedication took place at the reunion held June 28, 1986. Over 450 members and wives attended.

OFFICERS AND DIRECTORS
99th BOMB GROUP HISTORICAL SOCIETY
1989-1990-1991

Bill Smallwood, President
Fred Hueglin, Vice President
Walter Butler, Treasurer
George Coen, Historian/Editor
Chris Christiansen, Secretary

DIRECTORS

1989-1990	1990-1991
Bob Bacher	Bob Bacher
Dick Dempsey	Harvey Jennings
Jules Horowitz	Rex Carnes
Ken Kellstrom	Ken Kellstrom
Charles Miller	Leonard Hopen
Jeff Waguespack	Jeff Waguespack
	Roy Worthington
	Jules Horowitz

Our reunions began in 1957. The first was held at Sioux City, Iowa. Other Presidents not mentioned above are as follows:

Lewellyn Boatwright
Bernice Barr
George Coen
Joe Chance
Harvey Jennings

Many of the above Presidents served more than one year. They also served in other capacities, such as: Vice President, Treasurer, Editor, Historian, Secretary and gave many hours of their time preparing the newsletter for mailing to our members.

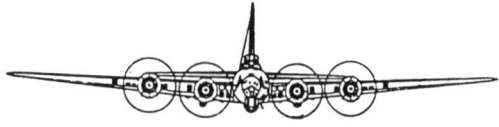

99th BOMBARDMENT GROUP

Constituted as 99th Bombardment Group (Heavy) on 28 Jan 1942. *Activated* on 1 Jun 1942. Trained with B-17's. Moved to North Africa, Feb-May 1943, and assigned to Twelfth AF. Entered combat in Mar 1943 and bombed such targets as airdomes, harbor facilities, shipping, railroads, viaducts, and bridges in Tunisia, Sardinia, Sicily, Pantelleria, and Italy until Dec 1943. Received a DUC for performance on 5 Jul 1943 when the group helped to neutralize fighter opposition prior to the invasion of Sicily by penetrating enemy defenses to bomb planes, hangars, fuel supplies, and ammunition dumps at the Gerbini airfield. Assigned to Fifteenth AF in Nov 1943 and moved to Italy in Dec. Flew long-range missions to attack such strategic objectives as oil refineries, marshalling yards, aircraft factories, and steel plants in Italy, France, Germany, Poland, Czechoslovakia, Austria, Hungary, Rumania, Bulgaria, Yugoslavia, and Greece. Received another DUC for withstanding severe fighter assaults to bomb the vital aircraft factory and facilities at Wiener Neustadt on 23 Apr 1944. Other operations included assisting ground forces at Anzio and Cassino, Feb-Mar 1944; participating in the pre-invasion bombing of southern France, Aug 1944; and supporting the Allied offensive in Po Valley, Apr 1945. *Inactivated* in Italy on 8 Nov 1945.

Redesignated 99th Bombardment Group (Very Heavy). Allotted to the reserve. *Activated* on 29 May 1947. *Inactivated* on 27 Jun 1949.

SQUADRONS. *346th:* 1942-1945; 1947-1949. *347th:* 1942-1945; 1947-1949. *348th:* 1942-1945; 1947-1949. *416th:* 1942-1945; 1947-1949.

STATIONS. Orlando AB, Fla, 1 Jun 1942; MacDill Field, Fla, 1 Jun 1942; Pendleton Field, Ore, 29 Jun 1942; Gowen Field, Idaho, 28 Aug 1942; Walla Walla, Wash, c. 30 Sep 1942; Sioux City AAB, Iowa, 17 Nov 1942-3 Jan 1943; Navarin, Algeria, c. 23 Feb 1943; Oudna, Tunisia, 4 Aug 1943; Tortorella Airfield, Italy, c. 11 Dec 1943; Marcianise, Italy, Oct-8 Nov 1945; Birmingham Mun Aprt, Ala, 29 May 1947-27 Jun 1949.

COMMANDERS. Unkn, Jun-Sep 1942; Col Fay R Upthegrove, c. Sep 1942; Lt Col Wayne E Thurman, 24 Nov 1943; Col Charles W Lawrence, 19 Dec 1943; Lt Col Wayne E Thurman, 26 Jan 1944; Col Ford J Lauer, 15 Feb 1944; Col Trenholm J Meyer, Jul 1944; Lt Col James A Barnett, Aug 1944; Col Ford J Lauer, Sept 1944; Col Raymond V Schwanbeck, Jan 1945; Lt Col Robert E Guay, 8 Oct 1945; Maj Joseph D Russell, 11 Oct 1945; Maj John S Giegel, 16 Oct 1945-unkn.

CAMPAIGNS. Air Combat, EAME Theater; Air Offensive, Europe; Tunisia; Sicily; Naples-Foggia; Anzio; Rome-Arno; Normandy; Northern France; Southern France; North Apennines; Rhineland; Central Europe; Po Valley.

DECORATIONS. Distinguished Unit Citations: Sicily, 5 Jul 1943; Austria, 23 Apr 1944.

INSIGNE. *Shield:* Azure, issuant from sinister chief a cloud argent emitting a lightning flash to dexter base or between an eye of the second with pupil sable represented as a radar scope of the third with eyelid of the like, and a globe of the last with lines of the fifth encircled by a motion picture film silver. *Motto:* SIGHT WITH MIGHT. (Approved 3 Nov 1943. This insigne was replaced 7 Feb 1958.)

We must not forget the Reunion Committees who worked countless days and months to make each reunion a memorable occasion for all.

While many other 99th members contributed significant time in starting the 99th Bomb Group Historical Society, I would be remiss if I omitted one tireless worker.

Bernie Barr, a stalwart of our group. I was given permission by Bernie to reprint the story appearing in our May, 1994 publication.

LUCKY MAN — 99th BOMB GROUP

Bernie Barr flew a nearly unheard 100 missions as a World War II bomber pilot.

99th Bomb Group Historical Society Newsletter Editor, Bernie Barr

WW II PILOT BEAT ODDS OF SURVIVAL

By John Fleck, Journal Staff Writer

If it can be said that history is written by those who survive it, then Bernie Barr is qualified. At his Northeast Heights home, the retired Air Force colonel——former Kirtland Air Force Base commander and veteran of a nearly unheard of 100 missions as a World War II bomber pilot—— still has his notes on a 3 by 5 pad, from a June 2, 1944 briefing.

The operation was called "Frantic Joe", an unprecedented international mission in which a swarm of allied bombers converged into a massive attack force on a target in Hungary, then flew on to land in the Soviet Union.

They then flew a return mission, bombing a Nazi target on their way back to their home bases. It was the first time foreign forces had been permitted to operate from Soviet soil.

His notes recall the radio frequencies, the target's name, compass headings, bomb fuse settings, the code words, the aircraft positions. Looking back, Barr also remembers the spectacle of that massive flight of aircraft—and the nagging fear.

"There was a certain feeling of safety in being part of such a great number of airplanes joining together," Barr wrote recently in The 99th Bomb Group Historical Society Newsletter. "But at the same time there was the apprehension of getting into an airplane that was easily to become the target of someone shooting live ammunition at you."

One-hundred times Barr felt apprehension—a 50 mission tour of duty in the Pacific Theater, followed by a stint in the United States, and then a second 50 mission tour of Europe.

Through 100 missions, Barr must acknowledge, the laws of probability ran against him surviving the war.

"The usual score was something like 10 or 15," said an admiring Walter Beckham, an Albuquerque friend of Barr who is himself a retired WWII fighter pilot.

As they near the 50th anniversary of those missions, Barr and his fellow aging 99th Bomb Group veterans, the survivors, are recording the old history with an energy borne both out of excitement of the time and the need to remember and record the memories before they are lost.

In issue after issue, The 99th Bomb Group Historical Society Newsletter that Barr co-edits sifts through the documents and records the fliers' memories ——the dramatic and mundane, life and death.

The 99th Bomb Group Reunion - Rapid City, SD 1992

Rapid City, SD Reunion September 1992
***Left to right:* Bob Imrie, Jim Hayes, Jim Hager, Jim Bruno**

Rapid City, SD Reunion September 1992
Left to right: Jim Hayes, Merlyn Bruno, Mrs. Covert, Bob Imrie, Jim Hager

Ontario, CA Reunion September 1993
Left to right: Atty. Roger Lyons, His Father - Roger Lyons, Marion Larkin

Rapid City, SD Reunion September 1992
Left to right: Russell T. Jacobs, Bill Holt, Jim Bruno
Front: Mrs. Holt

The Bankheads at Peachtree City, GA
Left to right: Pat Bankhead, Capt. Bankhead, Merlyn Bruno

THE 99TH BOMB GROUP REUNION - ST LOUIS 1995
MEMBERS AND THEIR SQUADRONS SHOWN

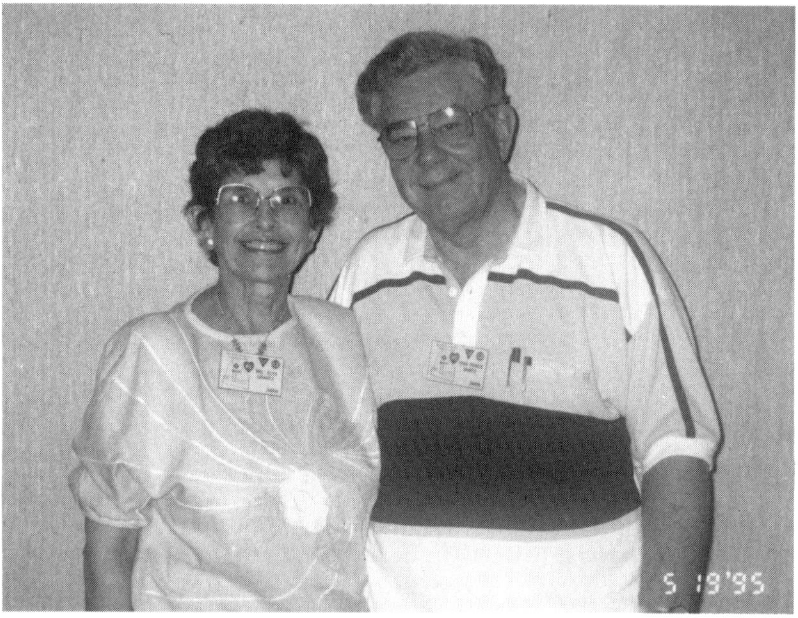

Our 1995 Hosts: Mr. and Mrs. Francis W. Grantz

Our 1994 Hampton, VA Hosts: Robert and Billie Bacher

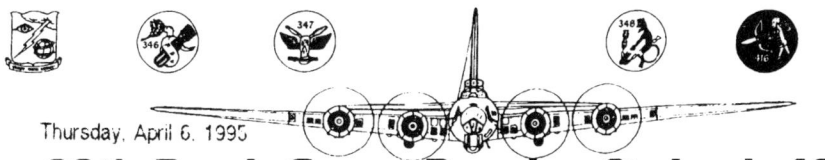

Thursday, April 6, 1995

99th Bomb Group Reunion-St. Louis 1995

Thursday, April 6, 1995

B James F. Bruno 347th Squadron
99th Bomb Group Historical Society
16645 Cherry Hill Drive
Brookfield, WI 53005-2716

Dear Jim:

Just a note to let you know that we have received your registration for the 1995 Reunion of the 99th Bomb Group Historical Society and your check for $ 180.

We look forward to your coming along with us for a GREAT Reunion here in St. Louis.

If you will be travelling by air and arriving at St. Louis Lambert International Airport, shuttle service for the Sheraton West Port Inn is available until 11 p.m. Use the courtesy phones by the luggage carousels for pick up service.

Travelling by car, the Sheraton West Port Inn is located in St. Louis County at the Interstate 270 and Page Blvd. Exit. Coming from the east: I-70, I-64, and I-55 lead to I-270, which is west of downtown about 20 miles. From the south, I-55 junctions at I-270 north to Page Blvd. From the west take I-64/US 40 east or I-70 east to I-270. Page Blvd. lies between I-64/US 40 and I-70.

If there are questions you may have or help is needed, please call 314-394-3314. Our concern is to help make this Reunion both memorable and enjoyable. St. Louis is a great city and we welcome you!

Cordially
99th BGHS Reunion - St. Louis 1995

Personal greetings!

Francis W. Grantz, host

Francis W. Grantz, Host • 15655 Clayton Road • P.O. Box 1125 • Ballwin, Missouri 63011-1125

Terry Barton and Wiliam Henderson
416th Squadron

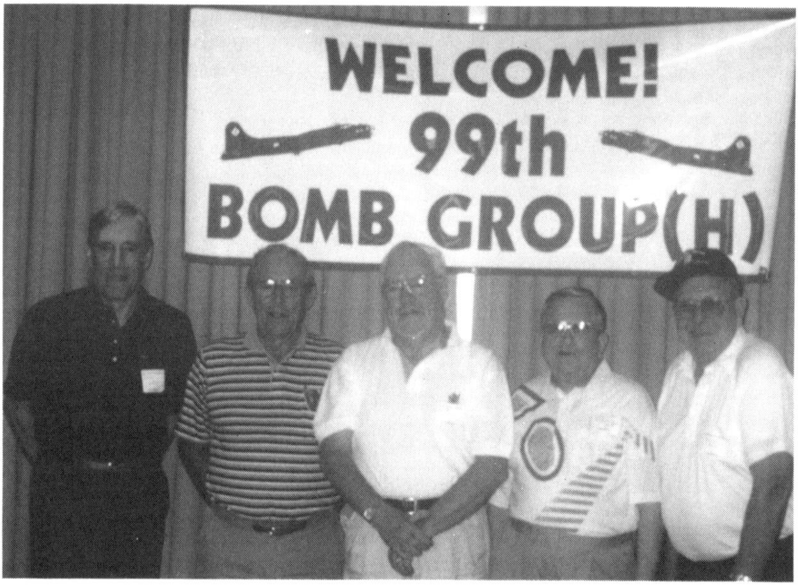

Links Crew
Left to right: Duane Cultra, Co-pilot; Lyle Link, Pilot; Alex Irwin, Engineer; Gordon Fletcher, Tail Gunner; George Ritter, Ball Turret Gunner. All 348th Squadron.

Mr. and Mrs. Warren B. Whitmore
348th Squadron

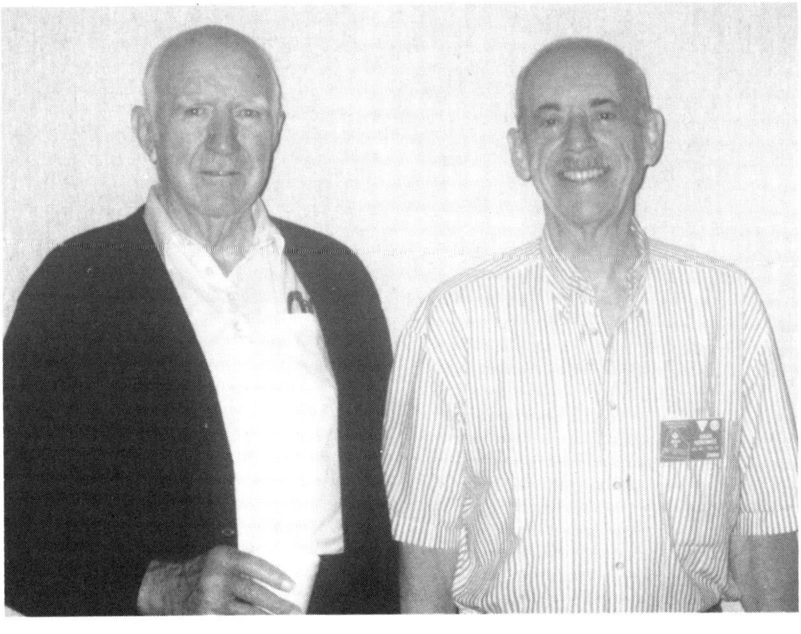

Bernie S. Barr - 416th and HQ Squadron Julius Horowitz - 348th
Squadron President (1993 and 1994)

Mr. and Mrs. Lew Boatwright
347th Squadron

Pilot Class of 42-I Advancsd Twin Engine
Roswell, NM Sept. 29, 1942

Seated - James Harmon Hayes *Left to right:* Charles F. Downey - 348th, James F. Bruno - 347th, William H. Holt - 347th, James S. Hager - 347th, Terry R. Barton - 416th, Marion J. Larkin - 346th (All completed 50 missions out of North Africa in 1943)

Left to right: Rex Greathouse - 346th, Morton Magee and Mrs. Magee - 348th, Denzel (Arkie) Clark - 348th, Julius Horowitz - 348th, Betty Clark - (Honorary)

Our group visited Scott Air Force Base, an Areomed Evacuation Unit. *Left to right:* Beyond Fighter Escort Author, James F. Bruno; Margie Leiby, Fred Leiby - 347th; Merlyn Bickford Bruno, Louis E. Walker, 346th.

Fred Lieby, Navigator, became a prisoner of war. He and Mrs. Leiby together with a group of former prisoners visited the camp in Germany in early May, 1995.

Louis Walker, Tail gunner bailed out of his B-17 that caught fire when the tail section fell off from the fuselage. His pilot, Lt. Hunter and eight crew members perished in the burning crash. (Louis has refused to sell his story to writers and agents.)

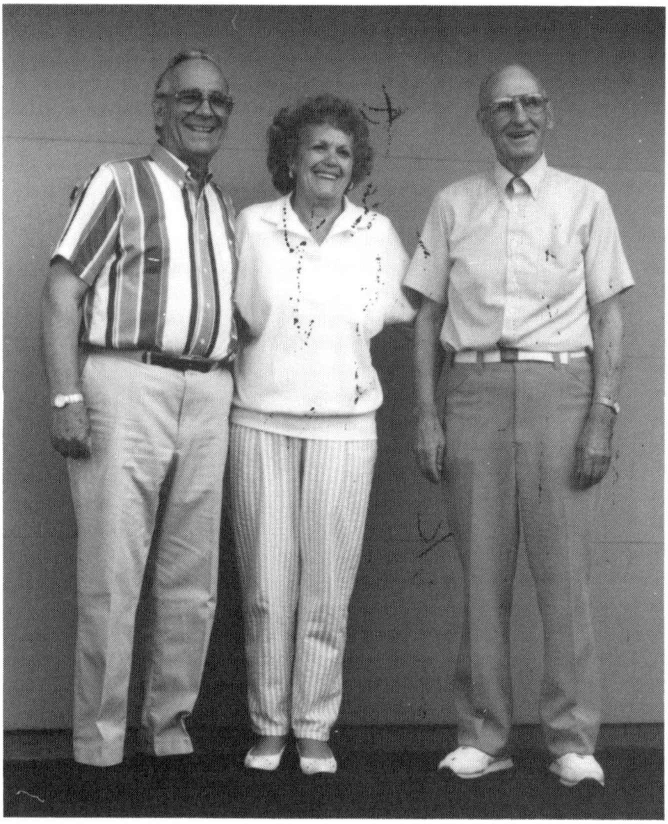

Found, Melvin Hall *(right)* in 1994. He came to Brookfield, WI where his niece, Kay Brooks and her family resides.

CHAPTER 20

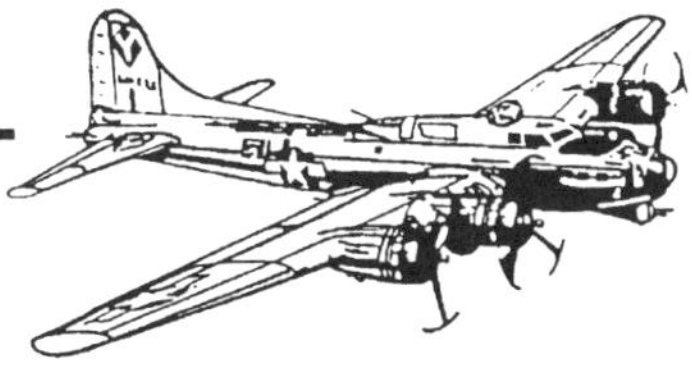

The Military, Still a Great Career Choice

Through the years the military has been the premier organization in our society when it comes to having a level playing field "where you can get to the top on how hard you are willing to work and your intelligence rather than the color of your skin or choice of religion." (Air Force Times, August, 1944)

After my third year in the Air Corps, I was Operations Officer at Ellington Field, Houston, Texas, one of the largest in the training command. My job classification called for the rank of Major. Promotions were frozen as the war in Europe was coming to an end.

My decision to take an early discharge was offered after the defeat of the Axis powers in Europe. It was the wrong move on September 13, 1945. As I was clearing the post an order came through stating all operations officers were to be sent to Bryan, Texas, their top instrument flying school. I lost that opportunity. Airlines asked prospective pilots if they had the "Green Card" from Bryan, Texas. I had to answer "No."

I was not happy with a remark the chief pilot at Northwest made during my visit. "You people bailed out when you got in trouble," he said. Commercial planes carried no parachutes for the pilots or passengers. Did he think I would free fall from whatever altitude trouble began? He also remarked they were awaiting the return of their pilots in the ferry command. The application he handed to me is filled out and yellowed with time in my desk drawer these past 50 years.

I asked for an instructing job of my former civilian instructors.

One was now a C.A.A. examiner and part owner of the flying school. I was denied my rating as they found flaws in my test. These men hated the military. Some ten years earlier they had been denied pilot training as they had not received a high school diploma. My insurance agent recommended me to an insurance adjusting company. Pay was $150.00 per month. Promotions were denied as I had not attended college.

I found myself trapped in a low paying job. Instructors were making $450.00 per month.

The $ 3,000.00 my wife and I had saved was spent the first year to maintain my family. The next year I had to sell my 1941 Pontiac.

Yes, the military had a level playing field. I found out the hard way!

Three pilots from my 347th squadron also left the military and tried the civilian work force and lifestyle.

One was squadron commander Harry R. Burrell. Upon calling on his mother in 1968, I was informed he had passed away. Harry, she told me was unable to find rewarding work. With the recommendation of Col. Upthegrove, he was accepted back into the regular army air corps. He moved up to the Strategic Air Command. He became the squadron commander of a B-47 bomber group in England during the Cold War.

Upon his return to the States, he served at the Pentagon and was Commander of Langley Air Force Base in Virginia and was up for promotion to Brigadier General when cancer caused his untimely death at age 49.

MAJOR GENERAL WILLIAM H. HOLT

Flying Cadet Classmate, William H. Holt, separated from the service after V.J. Day to return to civil aviation. He had obtained a commercial pilot's License before WWII but had jumped at the opportunity to fly "Big Time" military aircraft for Uncle Sam. His single desire was to fly fighters, but that didn't work out initially. However, after completing his combat tour in B-17s he requested assignment to the Ferry Command located at Long Beach, California where there was opportunity to ferry fighter aircraft produced on the West Coast. He accumulated all the fighter time and experience he could, which of course was not only satisfying but providential later.

Civil aviation was both enjoyable and profitable in those days of a pleasant and simple lifestyle. Bill took advantage of every flying opportunity, instructing, crop dusting, non-scheduled DC-3 airline and production test pilot on the Ryan Navion. But it soon became very apparent that something was missing, the security blanket of medical and monetary protection for his family in event of emergencies and a good retirement pension if all went well. Accordingly, he began the arduous task of applying for recall to the Air Force and the solicitation of recommendations on his behalf. It was on a trip to Washington, D.C. to demonstrate the Ryan Navion that, quite by coincidence, he was able to make an "in person" solicitation for recall. He was told "Your Orders will be out before you return to the West Coast." That was Gospel; Orders to Japan were there. Thirty months after leaving the Air Force he was back in.

Major General William H. Holt

42-1 classmate, September 29, 1942
(Now retired residing in San Diego)

Arriving in Japan, it was assignment time again. Bill's four engine B-17 time was now offset by his "fighter experience' in the Ferry Command and a strongly emphasized desire for a "fighter group" assignment. He prevailed and was soon in the 8th Fighter Group at Itazuki. After flying P-51s for 18 months prior to the Korean War and P-80s and P-84s in Korea, Bill's experience in fighters was established. Returning to the U.S., his Orders sent him to Air Defense Command fighters for 5 years. He subsequently was assigned to Great Britain where he flew both air defense and tactical fighters. Along the way from Japan to England, promotions from Major to Colonel were made. Back in the U.S., assignment was to Tactical Air Command and flying more fighters including the F-105 which led to a tour in South East Asia. Completing the sea tour Bill was assigned to the Pentagon for 3 years in fighter related positions. Promotions to Brigadier General and assignment to Europe in 1969 followed. In 1970 he was promoted to Major General. In 1974, he retired, pleased with the accomplishment of working into fighters.

H.B. (BUD) BANKHEAD

My first pilot, H. B. Bankhead, also took a discharge after the end of the war. He found a level playing field at Chicago-Southern Airlines, thanks to a 99th pilot, Bill Copsey, who was already flying there and gave him a tip they were hiring. Flying co-pilot in DC-3's with a pay of $165.00 per month was not a living wage. Fighting the war paid much better.

But then look at the pick of lovely stewardesses he had! Bankhead and his wife, Pat, a former Chicago-Southern stewardess and later with Delta, have three lovely daughters and wonderful grandchildren.

Chicago-Southern was bought out by Delta Airlines and Bankhead worked up to 4-engine jetliners and became one of the top 100 pilots out of over 4,000 being under employment.

Upon his mandatory retirement at age 60 he was Captain of the wide body L-1011, the pride of the Delta fleet.

Since retirement, Bankhead can be found wheeling his golf cart around Atlanta and more recently around the many golf courses in Peachtree City. In Peachtree City, Georgia people go visiting and shopping in their golf carts. Over 60 miles of asphalt trails wind through the subdivisions.

Having participated in many tournaments and filling a room full of trophies, H. B. Can truly be called the "Ben Hogan" of Peachtree City.

In 1994, Bankhead won the Rico Andreoli Memorial Golf Trophy. It is the trophy for the golfing circuit of the organization, "Retired Delta Pioneers" He will be defending his trophy in 1995. Good Luck Bankhead!

CHAPTER 21

A Pilot's Past

When I arrived, Jim Bruno greeted me with a smile. He was wearing a light-colored sweater with slacks, an outfit which gives a clue about his easy-going, friendly personality. With the exception of grey hair, for a man in his seventies, Jim has well-retained his youthful looks, as well as attitude. As we stepped into his small office, it became clear to me that Jim was prepared for this interview; he had all kinds of information that I might need—papers, pictures, and maps—at hand, most of which he had previously put together for the book he recently wrote about his experiences. Jim offered me his desk chair, cleared a space on the desk, and settled himself across from me. There we began our interview. I wasn't surprised at all to learn that, as most kids do at age nine, Jim Bruno wanted to fly. Unlike the rest, however, when he grew up, he did. "I wanted to fly ever since I was nine years old, when Lindbergh flew over Waukesha," Jim recalls. He knew then that one day he would be in the cockpit of an airplane. What he didn't know was how he would eventually turn this dream into a service for his country.

Between the time he was nine and the time he started high school, Jim kept this dream in mind. He graduated in 1937, having written his high school career book on aviation. One year later an essay he wrote on the importance of aviation to the U. S. Military was one of the winners of a national journalism contest. At age twenty-one, a year after the contest, Jim had his first flying lesson at the Waukesha County Airport—his dream had come true.

When Jim was twenty-two he and a friend decided to purchase a Curtis OX-5 Pheasant Bi-plane. A short time later Jim bought his friend's share, and at last he had his own set of wings. It wasn't until a member of the House of Representatives, and brother-in-law of a good friend suggested that they apply for U.S. Army Air Corps (now the U.S. Air

Force) that Jim even considered that option. The idea sounded like a good one though, and Jim decided to go for it.

Because he only had his high school diploma, he was required to pass a "rigid" physical, as well as a three-day college test, which he did in September of 1941. The Army called him in to report to Santa Ana, California, for pilot training five months later. There, he began "primary" training. After graduating from that, it was on to "basic flying school" and, finally, to "twin-engine advanced" training. During training, Jim flew various types of planes, including a Cessna, which was covered with bamboo and fabric.

A 1942 Graduation from Air Corps training left Jim with three choices of what to do with his new knowledge: go to Denver to fly P-38's for photo-reconnaissance (flying over after bombings to photograph the damage done), go to California to ferry supplies, or go to Salt Lake City to the Second Air Force. Jim's friend suggested they take the third option, and Jim complied.

When they got there, they were completely surprised to be sent off to Boise, Idaho for B-17 bomber training. Jim laughs, "So I got into bombers because the best man at my wedding suggested we go to Salt Lake City, never knowing we were going to bombers of course." For two months, Jim underwent B-17 training in Idaho, followed by two more months of training in Washington, and still more in Iowa. It wasn't until February, 1943 that Jim and his fellow graduates picked up their planes at Salinas, Kansas and prepared to go overseas. They flew to North Africa, and trained there for a couple more weeks before they were, at last, ready to begin their required fifty missions. Jim sums up the reason for the many months of training and practice by saying, "Each man was to be so proficient in his job that no man would endanger the entire crew."

Using his hands to help him explain, Jim gave me an idea

of where the ten people in their plane were and what they each did. He adds that most of the time he filled the position of co-pilot. The first mission Jim and his nine fellow crew members flew was over Sardinia. The bombings that can be attributed to them, however, also included Sicily, North Africa, France, and Greece. Austria would have made the list as well, but their plane was having engine problems that day, forcing them to turn around.

To me, it seemed as though there would be reason for at least a little fear during these bombing missions. Jim, on the other hand, after thinking carefully, index finger positioned on his temple, couldn't recall any particular instance in which he was especially scared. In fact, when I asked if he was ever concerned about the personal dangers involved in flying bombers, his response was a quick and simple, "Never came to mind." As for attitudes toward the use of bombs, and the war in general, Jim says that he and the rest of the crew were all just "gung-ho! We were young and really didn't think of it any other way. The crew had trained so well that we didn't think anything would bother us, at least most of the time."

On one mission in particular, Jim remembers everyone feeling a little reluctant. This was May 9, 1943—Mother's Day. That day, the idea of dropping bombs did bother Jim, because instead of dropping them on harbors or the usual, they were directly over the city of Palermo, Sicily. Originally, they had planned to bomb the harbor, but there were anti-aircraft guns in the city, and they needed to take out as many of these as possible. Jim becomes quieter and more pensive as he thinks back to this—the many civilians he's sure their bombs killed, and the plane they lost that day. In a section he wrote for his book, Jim says, "This was one morning we did not have our hearts in our work...."

Jim's most vivid memory of the times he spent in bombers was their sixteenth mission, over Messina, Sicily. This time they were "shot up pretty badly" by anti-aircraft guns, after which they still managed to fight off eight to ten fighters without any help from their flight leader; who, as Jim says, knew they were in trouble but did not drop back to help like he should have. Their plane had lost one propeller and some control, and almost an hour later they met up with a German fighter which they fought for twenty minutes. Eventually, they were able to land in Tunis, but by midnight the radio operator, having been hit by a cannon shell, had died.

At the close of our interview, I asked Jim to give me one word to describe his feelings every time he got into the B-17 and prepared for a mission. The answer I got regardless of the occasional times when things didn't go quite right, was "Happy." Jim has no regrets about the time he spent serving his country; he's proud of the job he did. There's no doubt in my mind that, given the chance, he would go the same route. Jim retired from the Air Force twenty-three years ago, but will always remember the dream he had as a child, and how it became important not only to him, but also to his country.

The Interviewer, Ami Jacobs graduated Summa Cum Laude from Cedarburg, WI High School in 1994.

Richard W. Cass, PH.D. Chair, English Dept. wrote me for my assessment of the interview.

I wrote; Ami is the next Barbara Walters. Ami is in modeling school, and - my stepgrandaughter.

Daughter Mary Kay and Family. Now Mrs. John Russom, granddaughter, Erin Ann and grandson, Sean Alan.

Sean Alan Russom
Now smiling in his World Series uniform

Merlyn - 1995

Merlyn and I were married in June, 1992

Merlyn's Family

Left to right:

Back row - Daniel L. Apple, D.V.M., Iowa State; Gordon J. Apple, JD, University of Wisconsin

Front row - Darla J. Heaviland, Ex. Secretary; Siegrid M. Fredrickson, MBA, University of Wisconsin; Barbara A. Jacobs, R.E. Broker

EPILOGUE

In the past 27 years since my trip to Omaha, Nebraska and being shown the three large scrap books about Harry R. Burrell by his Mother, this book began to take place. I have written many letters, read many stories and answered many letters. Time after time I kept wondering, why did this war have to happen? Why did it last so long? Why did so many men have to die?

A sobering Air Force story from the Omaha World Herald was hard to believe. They gave me permission to use it.

Air Force Hit Hardest In War.
Records Reveal Casualties Higher Than Any Other Branch Of Service.

26 October, 1945

Washington - U.S. air forces suffered a higher percentage of losses than any other branch of the service, according to Lt. Gen. Ira C. Eaker, deputy commander of the air forces. He revealed in part the costly price American airmen have paid when he reported that in 14 months of operations in Italy, the 15th air force lost 2,270 heavy bombers and 22,700 men. This the general explained was 115 percent of strength and added that "few can point to higher casualties."

Let us not forget our men of the Eighth Air Force out of England. In talking to my good friend Col. Harry Cruver and Dr. Harry Crosby, (Cruver the Commander of the 100th Bomb Group, Crosby, its lead navigator, and author of a great book, *A Wing And A Prayer*) I learned they had over 350,000 personnel and operated out of 112 air bases in England.

We Americans are well aware too many of our Army, Navy, Marines and Airmen gave their all for the freedom we are living today. Our prayers go out to loved ones we lost. God hears them all.